The discursive analysis of ideology [...] ideology mobilizes. In his new pat[...] rates on the formal structure of enjo[...] the Right. The enjoyment mobilize[...] resentment, it leaves behind the mo[...] ates racism and sexism. *Enjoyment I* classic – it cuts into the very heart o[...] and its apparent opposite, permissive liberalism.

C000157254

—Slavoj Žižek
Author of *Less Than Nothing*

McGowan's game-changing book compellingly answers one of the most vexing questions of our time: why do our best-intentioned leftist political projects continually fail? Against the contemporary progressive zeitgeist of championing the particular over the universal and insisting on inclusivity over nonbelonging, McGowan shows that emancipatory politics requires that we commit ourselves to accept our universal nonbelonging. Through his characteristically novel analyses of wide-ranging cultural and political phenomena—including the Black Lives Matter movement, sports fandom, the Christmas movie genre, the Haitian Revolution, and falling in love—McGowan obliges us to recognize that a truly egalitarian society is not possible without radical enjoyment.

—Jennifer Friedlander
Author of *Real Deceptions*

Forget political "opinions," to say nothing of "considered" opinions. In what deserves to be a game-changer, Todd McGowan convincingly shows how political postures are founded on forms of "enjoyment," unconscious gratifications paradoxically closer to suffering than to pleasure, closer to sacrifice than to satisfaction. A real adventure of insight.

—Richard Boothby
Author of *Embracing the Void: Rethinking the Origin of the Sacred*

McGowan's readability...is traceable to his ability to relate abstruse ideas to aspects of everyday life and common experiences. His style of writing when offering explanations for difficult terms and ideas results in an admirable lucidity.

—Sean Sheehan
Reviewing *Emancipation After Hegel* in *Marx and Philosophy*

Enjoyment
Right&Left

Todd McGowan

Enjoyment Right & Left

First Published by Sublation Media 2022
Copyright © 2022 Todd McGowan

All Rights Reserved
Commissioned and Edited by Douglas Lain
Copy Editor Konrad Jandavs

A Sublation Press Book
Published by Sublation Media LLC

Distributed by Ingramspark

www.sublationmedia.com

Print ISBN: 979-8-9867884-0-1
eBook ISBN: 979-8-9867884-1-8

Edited and typeset by Polifolia in East Germany

For Jennifer Friedlander and Henry Krips
Thanks for really lacking

Contents

Acknowledgments

I appreciate Douglas Lain having confidence in this book and encouraging me to publish it with Sublation Press.

My parents, Sandi and Bob McGowan, taught me the power of an unrelenting fundamentalist enjoyment throughout my early childhood. It was real horrorshow. But at the same time, they were unconsciously zealous devotees of German Idealism, which opened up a different path, one that I ended up choosing.

Thanks to Wyk McGowan for remaining friends with the three.

Jane and Del Neroni somehow came up with Hilary, without whom I would exist in total barrenness. Thus, I owe more to them than to anyone.

Thanks to my twin sons, Dashiell and Theo Neroni, who demonstrated to me the appeal of enjoying through one's enemy. Unfortunately, that enemy was typically me.

Certain people have made the University of Vermont more enjoyable for me than it is for most: Sarah Alexander, Andrew Barnaby, Emily Bernard, Bill Falls, John Waldron, and Hyon Joo Yoo.

Bea Bookchin is, for me, the absolute embodiment of leftist enjoyment. She manages to win friends and influence people even among her most entrenched political adversaries. She has never had an enemy, despite the best efforts of her allies.

LACK has been central to my experiences of excess. Thanks especially to Anna Kornbluh and Russel Sbriglia for reminding me that it can be enjoyable to read a novel every once in a while, as long as it's not written in the first person.

I appreciate the support of Clint Burnham, Joan Copjec, Matthew Flisfeder, Sheldon George, Scott Krzych, Don Kunze, Juan Pablo Lucchelli, Hugh Manon, Quentin Martin, Jonathan Mulrooney, Carol Owens, Kenneth Reinhard, Frances Restuccia, Molly Rothenberg, Stephanie Swales, Louis-Paul Willis, Jean Wyatt, and Cindy Zeiher. It's best not to have friends, but second best to have friends such as these.

Thanks to Sheila Kunkle for pointing out how the turn to the superego infects contemporary leftism. Her own resistance to superegoic pressure makes her the perfect friend of the id—and thus the perfect comrade.

Ryan Engley has talked through the problem of political enjoyment with me more than anyone else. But after all, he convinced me that sports provide a far more compelling terrain in which to invest ourselves psychically.

Slavoj Žižek has provided too much help. I appreciate that he always acted as if it wasn't a burden at all.

Walter Davis has rightly pushed my thinking at every turn to get beyond invoking enjoyment as an abstract category. As will quickly become evident, I continued to do it anyway just to annoy him.

Thanks to Jennifer Friedlander and Henry Krips for centering our friendship around existential despair. They are the ideal partners for founding an academic organization because they view all academic organizations with the proper amount of disdain. We share an abhorrence for the three Bs.

I'm not sure where Mari Ruti came from, but I am thankful for her absolute singularity of being. I feel as if her character calls me out with a summons of love to reinvent my soul. But I can't seem to be able to respond other than by opting out to try to preserve my immortal within.

I have a debt of gratitude for the friendship and intercessions of Richard Boothby, who knows that he knows nothing, unlike most of us, which is why my sons continually find him so much more interesting than me.

Thanks to Daniel Cho, whose reading of this book allowed certain ideas to quietly disappear from it. I feel badly for continuing to exploit his kind willingness to read through my books, but not badly enough to stop.

I appreciate Hilary Neroni having fewer critical comments on this book than others I have written. I thought this was a great sign until I realized that this book is simply much shorter than the others.

Thanks to Walter Davis, Paul Eisenstein, and Hilary Neroni, who remind me that we can make a heaven of hell and not just a hell of heaven.

1.

The
Outsiders

POLITICAL STRUGGLES TAKE PLACE to determine what form of enjoyment will predominate. And yet, neither political activists nor theorists tend to talk about enjoyment. It initially seems distant from politics, but when we recognize what's at stake in enjoyment, its importance for understanding politics will hopefully become clear. Enjoyment is not just pleasure but the experience that goes beyond pleasure—an experience of excess. There is always too much enjoyment, never just enough.[1] Because it is excessive, the path to enjoyment is unconscious. When we are caught up in it, we cannot consciously trace the reasons for why we are enjoying.[2] We enjoy when we unconsciously disturb our usual routines, throw ourselves off course, or cause too much trouble for ourselves. Such acts don't make sense according to conscious calculation. The inexplicability of enjoyment renders it a difficult political tool, which is why almost all political thinking has simply ignored it.

---

1 All enjoyment is troubling. The disturbance that it introduces is essential to its appeal, even though it is strange to view disturbance as appealing. There is no such thing as enjoyment that feels like it properly belongs to me. Instead, I experience it as if it were a foreign intruder.

2 Uncovering the structure of enjoyment is one of the tasks—perhaps the task—of psychoanalytic inquiry. This is why the attempt to uncover the political role that enjoyment plays must have constant recourse to psychoanalytic theorizing. It is the only theory that gives enjoyment priority within society and within the psyche.

To enjoy is to go beyond what fits within the confines of one's established social and psychic structure.[3] It is not simply the experience of eating an ice cream cone or buying a new car. Instead, it is continuing to eat ice cream cones after one is full or buying a car that one cannot afford. We enjoy what is not useful, what is not good for our health or well-being, what involves some sacrifice of what is good for us. Enjoyment is pleasure taken to the point that it becomes ruinous or at least damaging. But at the same time, this experience of enjoyment provides a reason to keep going in life, a motivation to get out of bed in the morning and engage with the world. When we enjoy, we touch on what exceeds everyday life and find the secret sauce that makes this everyday life bearable. Without any enjoyment at all, life would become so bland that we might not even be able to work up the enthusiasm for suicide. Enjoyment is always excessive—not just pleasing but also, crucially, disruptive. It manifests itself in the ecstatic religious experience, the devotion to a favorite sports team, the dedication to an unhealthy food, or the passion for a lover who portends certain heartbreak. The excesses of enjoyment don't confine themselves to personal life but define the political field as well. We see this enjoyment in massive political rallies, vehement protests, and outbursts of revolutionary (or reactionary) fervor. But it does not have an a priori status. Enjoyment is neither inherently positive or negative: its political and psychic valence depends on how we mobilize it.

Enjoyment is not only a large quantity of pleasure but pleasure that undergoes a transformation so that it becomes painful to

---

3   Alenka Zupančič ties enjoyment to what is missing within the symbolic structure. She writes, "the emergence of the signifying order directly coincides with the non-emergence of one signifier, and *at the place of this gap appears enjoyment* as the heterogeneous element pertaining to the signifying structure, yet irreducible to it." Alenka Zupančič, *What IS Sex?* (Cambridge: MIT Press, 2017), 53. The fact that enjoyment originates out of the gap in sense is what links it to the unconscious and renders it fundamentally incomprehensible. It stems from the point where there is no sense to be had.

bear.[4] Pleasures can be strictly pleasurable without an intermixture of pain, but one must suffer one's enjoyment. Enjoyment involves imposing an excess burden on oneself or creating excess excitation for oneself, whereas pleasure occurs with the elimination of this excess. The excessiveness of enjoyment gives it its potential political radicality. Enjoyment takes us out of our everyday existence. Because enjoyment goes beyond the possibilities present for me in my social position, it troubles not only me but also the social order itself. The way that a political protest might interfere with the flow of traffic stands as a synecdoche for the disruptiveness of enjoyment. Enjoyment involves going beyond the givens of the social order in a way that pleasure does not. While it might be pleasant to drive fast, it is enjoyable to block the traffic flow for the sake of protesting a new fuel tax.[5] Fast drivers keep things moving, while protests bring things to a stop. Or: pleasure fits, while enjoyment doesn't. This gives enjoyment its radical political charge relative to pleasure, which always relies on and leaves things as they are.

Politics gives a form to our enjoyment. Political campaigns offer the promise of a specific form of enjoyment to those who support them. This is why people have such an investment in politics and political struggle. It provides a way of organizing our enjoyment so that the possibility for this enjoyment appears maximized or the threat that others pose to it appears minimized. Enjoyment actually plays a determinative role in what a society looks

---

4   Although he objects to translating the French term *jouissance* with the English *enjoyment*, Néstor Braunstein clarifies the relationship between pleasure and enjoyment when he notes that enjoyment is "an excess intolerable to pleasure, now a manifestation of the body closer to extreme tension, to pain and suffering." Néstor A. Braunstein, *Jouissance: A Lacanian Concept*, trans. Silvia Rosman (Albany: SUNY Press, 2020), 14. The connection between enjoyment and suffering is crucial, and this is what is missing with pleasure.

5   The reference here is to the Gilets Jaunes (or Yellow Vests) movement in France, which began on November 17, 2018, as a protest against a new fuel tax levied by the Macron government.

like. One political leader might promise to allow people to take pride in and enjoy their nation by ridding it of outsiders. Another might offer the enjoyment of collective sacrifice to fight climate change. A third might propose completely transforming capitalist society into a communist alternative. A social order's political structure emerges out of a struggle between competing forms of enjoyment such as these. The struggle itself reveals the nature of these competing forms of enjoyment. We do not have to wait for the realization of the political program to grasp the operative form of enjoyment. It is apparent within the struggle itself. Every political position that people take up already demonstrates the form of enjoyment that they hope will prevail. How one enjoys defines how one functions as a political actor.[6]

Let's quickly look at the 2020 Presidential election in the United States. Donald Trump promised to sustain a nationalist and ethnocentric enjoyment that he successfully unleashed in his one term as president. He organized enjoyment through the slogan "Make America Great Again," which allowed partisans to enjoy the excesses of the American nation, to bask in the nation's worst transgressions without apology, and to believe in a definite racial hierarchy. Trump licensed acting without regard for the limitations that govern the social order. As a Trump supporter, one could beat up protesters with impunity, identify with racist police violence, or wear a baseball hat that would offend polite liberal society. To identify with Trump was also to enjoy his transgressions—one could vicariously "grab them by the pussy," swindle investors, hobnob with celebrities like Tom Brady, insult one's enemies without repercussions, and even partake in incestuous comments about his daughter's sex appeal. Trump's

---

6   We cannot separate a political struggle from the form that political power will ultimately take. How one fights is the index of how one will rule because the form of enjoyment that defines the struggle will necessarily carry over to the formation of the regime.

own transgressions turned him into a source of enjoyment for his followers. The transgressions did not detract from his appeal but were utterly central to it, since they provided the avenue for Trump supporters to enjoy in ways that they otherwise couldn't. His policies pushed this enjoyment even further.

When demonstrators marched against police violence toward the end of his term in office, Trump's response was to refuse to authorize any change in policing strategies, to blame protesters for causing problems, and to call for harsher treatment of suspects. Excessive policing provided enjoyment for Trump's followers because it involved unnecessary violence, violence that went beyond what any police officer need use to control a situation. This excessive police violence gave Trump supporters a path to enjoyment that they wouldn't have had without him and his embrace of the unruly police.

This excess also controlled the barrier between those who belonged and those who didn't, which is essential for the right-wing enjoyment that Trump proffered. The violence created the enjoyment of belonging for the Trump devotees because it forced others into the position of nonbelonging. Those drawing attention to the nation's racism or poverty rates revealed, for Trump and his followers, that they didn't properly belong to American society. Trump organized the enjoyment of his supporters around their belonging, which required highlighting that others didn't belong. One only feels as if one belongs when one has a group in sight that doesn't.

Anyone mentioning the nation's failures helped to constitute the group of Trump supporters by providing outsiders whom the group could enjoy hating. Their enjoyment depended on someone occupying the position of nonbelonging on the outside, someone who would not fit within the social field and thus could serve as a site of enjoyment. The key is that those on the Right didn't just disagree with their political opponents but experienced a feverish animus toward them. This feverish animus is the political enjoyment of the Right, an enjoyment that manifests itself in owning the libs or bashing political correctness. The Make America Great Again movement needed enemies who were holding America back from this supposed return to greatness, or else the movement itself would have lost its reason for existing and its mode of enjoying. It enjoyed through those it despised and through their position of nonbelonging. Trump promised the enjoyment of the nation as an ethnically homogeneous entity that had clear enemies in the advocates of political correctness. This term had a broad signification: it meant anything spoken to impugn the history of the United States or the structure of American society. You were being politically correct, in Trump's idiom, if you got in the way of real unapologetic American enjoyment with qualms about the nation's actions or those of its designated heroes.[7] The irony for Trump's form of enjoyment, like all right-wing enjoyment, is that it depended on those it vilified to nourish it. Right-wing enjoyment is fundamentally parasitic.

We can see an example of this in the fight against those who wanted to remove statues commemorating Confederate war heroes. To take down Confederate statues was to impede American enjoyment by damaging the ability to enjoy the excess of America's slaveholding past.[8] No one among Trump's supporters cared about the statues until someone tried to take them down. Conservatives were not flocking to pay homage to the statues prior to the moment they became politically problematic. The statues

---

7 Although the term *political correctness* remains in use, others have come to the fore to replace it in the lexicon of conservatives. One hears *critical race theory* or *wokeness* much more often than *political correctness*. In France, the term of art is *Islamo-Gauchisme* (Islamic Leftism).

8 The fact that the Confederate leaders were actually traitors to the United States reveals what's at stake in the attachment to them. It is a bond of enjoyment, a bond founded on a shared animus toward an egalitarian enemy. For the conservative supporter of Confederate monuments, their betrayal of the United States signifies their fidelity to the right-wing form of enjoyment.

had no practical value, and no one took pleasure in their aesthetic beauty, such as it was. But their excessiveness, their celebration of a past that no one could defend morally or logically, gave them an enjoyment value. What's crucial to see is that this enjoyment value only became palpable when the detractors threatened the continued display of the statues. The threat posed by those who would topple the statues allows their conservative champions to suffer—and thus to enjoy. The enjoyment value of the statues sent conservative activists marching into the streets to preserve them.[9] Had the statues only provided pleasure, their removal would have occasioned as much uproar as occurred when the statehouse bushes were trimmed. The enjoyment that Trump promised and proffered required an enemy, such as those taking down statues. The enemy gives the conservative a position that can function as a site to experience a disturbing enjoyment.

In response to Trump's ethnically homogeneous nationalism, Joe Biden appeared initially to offer a different way of structuring enjoyment. For Biden, there was enjoyment in simply returning to normal, which meant returning to capitalist society before the Trump presidency. His statement to European leaders, "America's back," typified this position. While just returning to normal seems to be a position relatively bereft of enjoyment, Biden's candidacy of reconstituted normality actually brought many to tears of enjoyment when it triumphed. Normality became a transcendent site of enjoyment after the Trump years, when corruption and

---

9   Hilary Neroni interprets Confederate signifiers and monuments as fetish objects that allow people to enjoy their racism while disavowing the suffering that it entails for others. She writes, "Taking the Confederate signs and names as a fetish object is a response to lack that allows people to disavow slavery while still repeating its psychic investment." Hilary Neroni, "Confederate Signifiers in Vermont: Fetish Objects and Racist Enjoyment," in *Lacan and Race: Racism, Identity, and Psychoanalytic Theory*, eds. Sheldon George and Derek Hook (New York: Routledge, 2021), 56. Fetishism facilitates an enjoyment that occurs without any conscious awareness of its source.

prevarication functioned as the standard. Despite his overall pedestrian qualities as a candidate (or rather because of these qualities), Biden came to embody the perfect alternative to the form of enjoyment that Trump offered. Biden presented people with their old political system as a new form of enjoyment, which is what led to Trump's defeat. His conjuration of restored normality as a way of organizing enjoyment managed to win more adherents than Trump's nationalism.

But Biden was not as different from Trump as this account might suggest. While he disdained Trump's racist nationalism and overt corruption, he took a tack remarkably similar to Trump by focusing on an enemy. One could promise the enjoyment of a return to normal only if one had a figure of abnormality to fight against. This figure was Trump himself. Trump became the outsider destroying the American system that Biden and his followers could enjoy hating. To support Biden was to enjoy through the excesses of Trump, whom one despised. This is one reason why Biden's support cratered soon after Trump's defeat. The unifying figure—the enemy that served as the source of enjoyment—had disappeared.

Although the contest between the enjoyment that Trump offers and what Biden counters with appears to have incredibly high stakes, their contest does not illustrate the divide between the forms of enjoyment that characterize Right and Left. The existence of Biden as the alternative reveals the bankruptcy of the contemporary Left, not just in the United States but around most of the world. While Trump might adequately represent a conservative form of enjoyment, Biden does not provide a revelatory emancipatory counterexample. The structure of enjoyment that he advocates bears too much of a resemblance to that of his opponent. His invocation of a return to normality falls short of an emancipatory mobilization of enjoyment that we might see at work in the Haiti of Toussaint Louverture, the Bolivia of Evo

Morales, or even the movement surrounding Bernie Sanders. There are radical differences in the structure of Right and Left enjoyment that the opposition between Trump and Biden (or Marine Le Pen and Emmanuel Macron in France) doesn't capture. In other words, we have to look beyond electoral battles if we want to see the different structures of enjoyment that conservative and emancipatory political movements offer. While the structure of rightist enjoyment has multiple manifestations in recent and contemporary political activity, we must strain our eyes to see the leftist form of enjoyment. Too often, the Left fails to distinguish itself vigorously enough from the Right.

By understanding the difference between Right and Left as the difference between competing forms of enjoyment, we can make sense of why right-wing movements seem to do a better job mobilizing people's emotions and why left-wing movements seem always ready to collapse. The advantages of the Right include control of more wealth, certainly, but they are also tied to the form of enjoyment that the Right accesses. Despite these structural advantages, the Right operates with an enjoyment that it cannot universalize, in contrast to that of the Left, which is inherently universalist.[10] Universality is the basis of the leftist emancipatory project. It leaves no one behind, whereas the rightist project depends on some not just being left behind but actively ostracized.[11]

---

10 Leftist insistence on universality does not imply the loss of the subject's singularity. It is through the recognition of the universal that we discover singularity. They are not at odds with each other. As Mari Ruti points out, "there is no necessary contradiction between the singularity of experience and the universality of ethical principles." Mari Ruti, *Distillations: Theory, Ethics, Affect* (New York: Bloomsbury, 2018), 26. By making clear an investment in universality, one is able to distinguish the singularity of the subject from its symbolic identity, which is just a result of its position in the social order. Universality gives one distance from one's given particular identity.

11 We should question the political allegiances of purported leftists who question universality. It is perhaps not a coincidence that Michel Foucault, one of the leading opponents of universalizing, spent a great deal of his life as

Right-wing enjoyment is necessarily provincial because it relies on an outsider that threatens it. The threatening outsider is not a contingent development that the rightist encounters but the sine qua non of right-wing enjoyment. The conservative position enjoys through this threat, which is why right-wing leaders constantly belabor the dangers posed by outsiders more than their own positive political program. This is not an accident. Their plans are empty of enjoyment without the outsider that threatens to undo them. Due to this formal requirement, rightist enjoyment excludes the possibility of bringing everyone together under a conservative umbrella. For this position to deliver the enjoyment that drives it, someone must play the heavy and not belong. Every conservative project demands an enemy in order to make it appealing to its adherents.

Despite their different forms, both rightist and leftist enjoyment have the same origin: every social order has contradictions that create points that appear impossible to inhabit from within the order itself. Enjoyment derives from these contradictions because they provide avenues for people to transcend the limits that the society lays down, avenues for them to be excessive. We are not just confined to the possibilities that the social order makes available to us. To enjoy is to eclipse these given possibilities. The contradictions of every social order create openings to enjoy, to go beyond what has been authorized. Enjoyment is an immanent transcendence—not an experience of the divine but one in which we transcend the limits that the social order establishes as constraints on what is possible. The social order is structured in such a way that certain positions cannot register in its accounting. Certain positions simply don't exist as social possibilities. But these social impossibilities represent points where we can enjoy.

Let's look at a straightforward example. The fundamental contradiction of American sexist society in the mid-twentieth

---

a Gaullist conservative, a fact that his theoretical descendants, for obvious reasons, seldom draw attention to.

century was to conceptualize the figure of the woman as both a nonsexual maternal figure and a sex object. Sexism operated through this division of the woman into two contradictory identities. If one was a nonsexual maternal figure, one could not simultaneously be a sex object. The two identities mutually excluded each other. And yet, this sexist society constituted female identity through these two identities, which put all women in a contradictory situation. Sexist ideology attempted to deal with this contradiction by dividing women into either mothers or sex objects. In this way, the contradiction ceased to appear as a contradiction and became an opposition between different people: some were mothers, while others were sex objects. The contradiction became obscured in particular differences between women, although the contradiction remained a problem that women had to address. The social order's fundamental contradiction created a point of impossibility—in this case, the maternal sex object. To occupy this contradictory position was to exceed the confines of sexist society. Such excess opened up a space for enjoyment. The emancipatory position, the stance of a leftist enjoyment, is to occupy the contradiction. Leftism discovers universality in the social contradiction where there is no recognition or authorization. This contradictory position is universal because it is available to everyone regardless of social status or political power.

This point of impossibility is socially impossible but not ontologically so, which is why one could run into sexualized mothers even within rampant sexism. The position that this sexist society deemed impossible was actually a real possibility, a position that one could take up in defiance of the prevailing social mandates. Within any social order, one can do the impossible and occupy the position that the social order deems nonexistent. But because occupying the impossible position brings the social contradiction to light, it entails ostracism and reprobation. The sexist society labeled the sexualized mother "unfit" or an "abomination" or a "slut." Or people who bought into this society collectively policed it by looking at her askance and trying to discipline her into an authorized identity. Such assaults indicated the threat that those who embraced the contradiction and occupied the impossible position posed to the oppressive social structure. Those who took up the position of the maternal sex object in sexist society occupied this society's contradiction and did the impossible. Embracing the contradiction in this way frees one from the dictates of social authority. It frees one to enjoy.

Enjoyment is possible in every social order because no social order is coherent and complete. Each is lacking. Each is beset by contradictions that emerge through its drive to constitute itself as a whole. If it were coherent and formed without any fissures, a social order would have no way to admit new members, which is a requirement for every society, even that of the Shakers, who disdained sexual reproduction but not social reproduction. In this sense, the limitations of the social order are necessary because they create the opening for new members. But they also provide a site for challenges to the order.[12]

A society constitutes itself as a whole by creating a barrier between itself and what is external to it. The contrast between inside and outside is essential for any society. This contrast manifests itself through the determination of belonging. A society depends on recognizing those who belong and withholding recognition

---

12 Louis Althusser's well-known theory of ideological interpellation explains how the social order incorporates new members by hailing them as subjects. For Althusser, this process succeeds even when—or especially when—a concrete individual misrecognizes itself as the subject of the ideological hail. Althusser never envisions a failed ideological interpellation. As a result, his explanation of the process of incorporating new members of the social order explains too much. The process must be able to fail if it is able to succeed. That is, the failure testifies to the society's openness to the outside, which is what enables it to accommodate new members. If ideological interpellation worked as well as Althusser theorizes, no society would ever be able to admit any new members.

from those who don't in order to define itself. The dividing line between belonging and nonbelonging is how a social order creates the semblance of coherence. Some social authority must exist to grant recognition and determine who belongs. But this is where the contradiction appears that opens up the possibility for enjoyment. The contradiction creates a space that doesn't fit within the regime of signification, a space of immanent transcendence. There is a contradiction within every social order due to the status of the authority that polices belonging.

The social authority that doles out recognition has its authority through the recognition that the members of the society give to it. An authority is an authority insofar as most people in the society treat it as one. Even in democratic countries, it is not the vote that authorizes the leader. It is the collective belief in the validity of the vote or whatever process determines who the authority will be. Although the people don't consciously make a collective decision to endow someone with authority, their authorization is nonetheless a necessary condition for the erection of a figure of social authority. This is the basic contradiction: the social authority that distributes recognition must itself be recognized by those to whom it grants recognition. An infinite regress emerges that prevents any social authority from having an authorized status.[13] The authority's authorization comes from those whom

---

13 Jean-Jacques Rousseau attempts to avoid the infinite regress of authorization through the notion of the general will. The general will embodies the collective spirit of the society and grants legitimacy to the leader through the support that it provides. In *The Social Contract*, Rousseau writes, "*Each of us puts his person and his full power under the supreme direction of the general will; and in a body we receive each member as an indivisible part of the whole.*" Jean-Jacques Rousseau, *The Social Contract*, in *The Social Contract and Other Later Political Writings*, ed. Victor Gourevitch (Cambridge: Cambridge University Press, 1997), 50. The problem with recourse to the general will is that Rousseau must assume that the general will itself is authorized. He fails to deduce its authority, which causes it to stand out as an unwarranted presupposition within his system.

the authority itself recognizes as having the power to authorize the authority.[14] As a result, there is no one with the authority to litigate between belonging and nonbelonging, to decide between who belongs and who doesn't. The line between inside and outside must be drawn, but there is no one authorized to draw it that doesn't receive this authorization from an ultimately unauthorized source.[15] This contradiction haunts every social order, no matter how secure its organizational structure seems to be.

This contradiction creates a porous social order, one populated by holes of nonbelonging that undermine its coherence. No one can be sure of belonging because there is no authorized authority that could ensure this belonging. As a result, one's social identity is never secure but always in question. One's place within the society is never certain but always on the verge of being lost. This means that everyone within a social order is virtually in the place of the sexualized mother within the sexist society—that is, in the position of nonbelonging—but people cling to the illusion of belonging in order to avoid coming to terms with this actuality. No one wants to confront their nonbelonging head-on, and yet it is precisely this nonbelonging that operates as the source of their enjoyment. Everyone relies on an unauthorized authority,

---

14 This inherent defect that undermines all authority stems from the structure of language in which authority must exercise itself. As Joan Copjec points out in *Read My Desire*, language is limited by its inability to signify itself, which renders authority unable to authorize itself. She states, "It is in the fact that a signifier is unable to signify itself but must always call on another in an infinite appeal to one signifier more, that language's internal limit is located." Joan Copjec, *Read My Desire: Lacan Against the Historicists* (Cambridge: MIT Press, 1994), 175. Just as there is no final signifier that nails down signification, there is no final authority that provides an authorization for the figure of authority.

15 The psychoanalytic term for the failure of every social authority is symbolic castration. There is no authority that escapes symbolic castration because there is no authority that doesn't rely on the recognition of those it recognizes.

but very few admit this to themselves. They cling instead to the apparent security that resides in belonging, but all belonging is ultimately illusory.

The unauthorized status of all social authority leaves the members of the society without any assurance of their belonging. I strive to belong, but no recognition or validation can assure me fully that I have achieved belonging. I am stuck trying to belong but never certain whether I do or not. Rather than being something to lament, it is precisely this failure to belong that opens up the possibility for enjoyment. If one could belong to a social order and know that one received recognition from the society, this secure recognition would rule out enjoyment. Full social recognition would entail a complete evacuation of enjoyment. Enjoyment derives from the failure of recognition, from the point at which the social order ceases to authorize one's position. This is the point of contradiction.

Contradiction is the necessary condition for enjoyment. It is through the empty spaces in the social order that contradiction opens up where subjects are able to enjoy themselves. Since enjoyment is the experience of excess, it occurs when one goes beyond the socially authorized space and takes up a position that doesn't fit within the map of the social order. Despite their clear appeal, we don't enjoy belonging and recognition, although we can take pleasure in them. Belonging and recognition confine us within a symbolic identity, stripping away all potential to enjoy. There is no enjoyment in fitting in. We enjoy the failure of the social order, the inability to fit in, the points at which we can go beyond the options that the society lays out for us and inhabit the unauthorized space of nonbelonging. Even though it's unpleasant not to fit in, it is enjoyable. All enjoyment emerges out of nonbelonging, from occupying the position of those who don't fit.[16]

---

16 Perhaps the most compelling literary depiction of the enjoyment that derives from not fitting in comes in Toni Morrison's *Sula*. The titular character fails to

Let's return to the example of the woman in the sexist society. One enjoyed in this society by inhabiting the contradiction, by refusing to decide between being maternal and being sexual but instead occupying both positions at once, which is what the feminists of the 1970s around the world did. Occupying the impossible position, the position of the social contradiction, involved an embrace of the contradiction. In this case, the women allowed themselves to be both maternal and sexual. By taking up this position, they highlighted the failure of the social order. Emancipation lives in the blank space within the society where enjoyment can emerge.

The space for enjoyment exists because the structure of language that undergirds the social order centers around what cannot be represented. Language doesn't aim at naming what we can perceive but what we can't. There is a hole within every language that marks this fundamental absence. This paradox of language holds the key to making sense of how the space for enjoyment emerges within the structure of signification. As Richard Boothby importantly states in *Freud as Philosopher*, "the innermost essence of language functions to evoke something that is missing in the object. In its most primordial function, language serves to name the no-thing. What most profoundly sets speech in motion is a dimension of absence in perception, a lack that haunts perceptual presence, a dimension of perception that remains uncognizable."[17] The impossible that cannot be represented is a structural necessity for language and thus for the social order. It is precisely this point of impossibility that highlights what gives our existence its worth. This point creates the opening for enjoyment, which occurs where the structure is at odds with itself and cannot account for what goes on.

---

meet the social expectations that all the other characters in the novel, including her best friend Nel, place on her. She enjoys, and the other characters who disdain her for her failure to fit in simultaneously feed off this enjoyment.

17 Richard Boothby, *Freud as Philosopher: Metapsychology After Lacan* (New York: Routledge, 2001), 217.

Enjoyment emerges when what cannot happen does happen. The contradiction inherent in this statement is the key to how enjoyment functions because it depends on contradiction. What the social order formally rules out and deems contradictory nonetheless takes place, even though it has no social authorization. The field of possibilities in any society always involves a contradiction—a point at which the society makes demands on people that are irreconcilable with each other—and this contradiction creates an impossibility or something that cannot happen within the existing social coordinates. Enjoyment is the experience of the impossible, which is why it has clear political implications.

The genuine political act must occupy the place of the impossible. Although many political struggles seem to involve conflicting possibilities—more or less taxes, universal or private health care, increased military spending or money for the homeless, communism or capitalism—the real political struggle focuses on what the social order characterizes as impossible. To do the impossible is to break from the field of given possibilities within a society and change the social coordinates.[18] When a political act accomplishes this, it achieves a transcendence relative to the field of possibilities, and this transcendence generates enjoyment. The radical political act is consonant with the radicality of enjoyment. We enjoy at the site of contradiction within the social order where we can do the impossible.

---

18 Slavoj Žižek is the great champion of the impossible as the domain of the political act. This idea receives its clearest articulation in *The Ticklish Subject*, where he states, "authentic politics is … the art of the *impossible*—it changes the very parameters of what is considered 'possible' in the existing constellation." Slavoj Žižek, *The Ticklish Subject: The Absent Centre of Political Ontology* (London: Verso, 1999), 199. For Žižek, to act politically is to act from a position that the controlling symbolic structure rules out. One goes beyond the given possibilities. It is only in doing so that one can, as Žižek suggests, make genuine political changes. What Žižek doesn't do is to connect the impossible act to the enjoyment of social contradiction.

In his theorization of decolonial struggle, Frantz Fanon describes several occasions when the impossible happens, when colonized subjects refuse the subservient position that the colonizer puts them in. This is, for Fanon, the essence of a leftist emancipatory struggle. By refusing the possibilities that colonialism presents, the colonized subject does what appears impossible according to the structure of colonial relations. In *The Wretched of the Earth*, he writes, "The colonized subject ... discovers that his life, his breathing and his heartbeats are the same as the colonist's. He discovers that the skin of the colonist is not worth more than the 'native's.' In other words, his world receives a fundamental jolt."[19] Occupying the position of the impossible—that of equality for the colonized subject—brings with it an influx of enjoyment. This enjoyment comes as a jolt for the oppressing colonizer, but, as Fanon makes clear, it is also a jolt for the colonized subjects themselves. This is what leftist enjoyment looks like.

To do the impossible in this sense is to occupy the point of contradiction within the social order. The colonial society deems the colonized to be unequal to the colonizers, but at the same time, the colonizers trumpet a creed of human equality. When the colonized actually assert their equality, they make this contradiction evident, as Fanon points out. The enjoyment of occupying the contradictory point within colonial society is a leftist enjoyment that portends the end of that society. Occupying this position accomplishes the impossible.

Doing the impossible creates a psychic disturbance. The enjoyment that it provides simultaneously deprives people of the symbolic coordinates that had hitherto given them the sense of a coherent identity. To occupy the position of social contradiction and do the impossible is to throw one's symbolic identity into disarray. One loses the illusory security of recognized belonging.

---

19 Frantz Fanon, *The Wretched of the Earth*, trans. Richard Philcox (New York: Grove Press, 2004), 10.

Even though this security is always illusory, it nonetheless provides a sense of stability and coherence. Enjoyment puts this aside. The enjoyment of the impossible is the enjoyment of a radical disruption of one's symbolic identity.

Because of its emergence through disruption of the established social order, enjoyment seems to tilt inherently to the Left. Enjoyment marks a threat to the ruling order because it doesn't fit properly within that order. But disruption is not always emancipatory. The Right is able to marshal enjoyment for conservative or reactionary purposes more easily than the Left does so for the sake of emancipation. Conservative forces can take the disruptiveness of enjoyment and use it to further a sense of belonging for some, as long as there are others who don't belong. For both Right and Left, enjoyment always has the same source: the contradictions of the social order where the site of nonbelonging manifests itself. But Right and Left do not respond to this enjoyment in the same way.

Leftism or the emancipatory project is the embrace of the radical enjoyment of contradiction, the enjoyment of nonbelonging. This is visible in leftist movements throughout human history, from the Spartacus revolt in ancient Rome to the Haitian Revolution to the Russian Revolution to the Dalit Buddhist movement in India to the Zapatista movement in Mexico to Black Lives Matter in the contemporary United States. The emancipatory project focuses on privileging the fact of nonbelonging and taking this nonbelonging as the model for the enjoyment it proffers.

The Haitian Revolution shows this logic perfectly. When Napoleon sent troops to Haiti to re-enslave the island after the successful revolution, the Haitian soldiers confronted the French not as enemies to be ruthlessly eliminated but as fellow participants in a universal struggle who had lost their way. They let the French know that they were fighting on the wrong side, that the Haitian side was that of *liberté*, égalité, and *fraternité*. This is what C. L. R. James recounts in a moving passage from *The Black Jacobins*. He writes, "The [French] soldiers still thought of themselves as a revolutionary army. Yet at nights they heard the blacks in the fortress singing the *Marseillaise*, the Ça Ira, and the other revolutionary songs."[20] The Haitian troops don't exclusively sing Haitian songs but also those of the French Revolution itself, thereby showing the invaders that the Haitian fight was a universal one and that the French invaders were caught up in a conservative particularist position.

This episode from the Haitian Revolution reveals what leftist or emancipatory nonbelonging looks like. It provides an opening for the adversary to join the struggle and absolutely refuses to place the adversary in the position of an enemy. What's more, it proclaims no exclusivity for itself. Neither blood, nor history, nor symbolic identity determines one's participation in the group of nonbelonging because this group has no barriers to keep people out. It is the group of those who are out.

Those who don't belong to the society and receive no recognition become the focus of the leftist movement. From the perspective of emancipation, these figures of nonbelonging are not exceptions to the rule but the paradigm for all subjectivity. The subject is defined by its failure to belong, its inability to fit within the assigned places that the social order lays out. This failure is what opens up the possibility of enjoyment. But those who attempt to belong to the social order flee their subjectivity into the promised coherent stability of a symbolic identity, which is precisely what is denied to the figures of nonbelonging, such as the colonized in Algeria when Fanon was there fighting for independence.

Whether it is slaves in Haiti or Dalits in India, emancipation recognizes that nonbelonging actually harbors all of the social order's enjoyment. It is not an exceptional position that we should strive to eliminate but the basic form of enjoying subjectivity that

---

20 C. L. R. James, *The Black Jacobins: Toussaint L'Ouverture and the San Domingo Revolution*, 2nd ed. rev. (New York: Random House, 1963), 317.

becomes obfuscated among those who strive to belong. Even though the people who are reduced to nothing but their nonbelonging have no social advantages and suffer tremendous oppression, they make evident the limits of the social order that emerge through its contradictions. Enjoyment emanates from the position of nonbelonging that social authority does not recognize. It is not just particular figures of nonbelonging that have the monopoly on this enjoyment. The enjoyment of nonbelonging is available to everyone because no one can assuredly belong. Recognizing the universality of nonbelonging is the emancipatory project.

By privileging the enjoyment of nonbelonging, emancipation tries to make clear the universality of nonbelonging. Rather than continuing to emphasize the distinction between those who belong and those who don't, the emancipatory project emphasizes that there is no belonging, that all belonging is an illusion sustained only through the contrast with nonbelonging. This is what Fanon is getting at when he describes the moment of emancipation when the colonized subject ceases to believe in the colonizer's difference. At this point, the figure of nonbelonging sees that belonging is illusory. This is a move that the colonizer must make as well: to give up the sense of belonging is the only path to emancipation. The leftist movement works through an identification with the figures of nonbelonging that attempts to make evident the universality of nonbelonging and thus realize the emancipatory project.

Nonbelonging is universal because everyone is a subject who fails to have a recognized symbolic identity. This is not just the destiny of the slaves in Haiti or the Dalits in India. Even the Haitian sugar plantation owners and the Indian Brahmins, the people on top in these societies, suffer from the failure of their symbolic identities to ensure their belonging. While their social situation is better than that of the slaves or Dalits—no Brahmin would want to trade places with a Dalit, to be sure—their identity is no more secure. No social recognition is ever adequate, even for those who seem to have the fullest form of recognition. No social authority can produce complete belonging because there is no authorized authority that itself doesn't need to be authorized.

The more one invests oneself in the project of belonging, the more one experiences the inadequacy of recognition and the failure of belonging. This is why those striving to belong need to emphasize the nonbelonging of others so vociferously. Such a move helps to secure their sense of belonging because it defines those who are in by distinguishing them from those who are out. But this is precisely what the emancipatory politics abjures. It has its basis in a tacit recognition of the failure of all social recognition and the resultant universality of nonbelonging. The universality of nonbelonging constitutes the emancipatory project. To grasp this universality collectively is to embrace emancipation.

The Left enjoys the social order's internal failure, no matter what the structure of that social order is. For the Left, the aim is to occupy the position of impossibility where the social contradiction occurs. This is a point of shared nonbelonging, a point that is part of the social order but doesn't belong to it. This positioning makes it the site where one can enjoy without the need for an enemy. The leftist form of enjoyment occurs through the collective failure to belong to the society and the collective embrace of contradiction. It is inherently universal because it doesn't rely on an enemy.[21] There is no leftism with an enemy.

---

21 The project of emancipation is universalist because it cannot leave some people out and remain emancipatory. Emancipation for some and not for others is not emancipation at all but a prescription for an oppressive society. While universality has gotten a bad name since the failure of the communist experiment in the twentieth century, it remains the foundation of the leftist project. A leftism that abandons universality for the emancipation of the particular has turned into its opposite. For more on the necessary universality of emancipation, see Todd McGowan, *Universality and Identity Politics* (New York: Columbia University Press, 2020).

The Right rejects the impossible contradiction and attempts to assert social belonging by contrasting those who belong with the enemy who doesn't. Conservatism offers the image of belonging to its adherents at the cost of relegating others to the position of nonbelonging. The enjoyment of this position derives from the enemy that doesn't belong. The rightist enjoys through the figure it despises because this figure brings the conservative in touch with the contradiction, which otherwise the conservative position seeks to avoid. The rightist illusion of belonging only becomes an enjoyable position to occupy when there is an enemy threatening it from the position of nonbelonging. Thus, right-wing politics is a project replete with enemies who provide it with the enjoyment necessary to fuel the project. The enemy of the Right is not just a contingent development but a necessary feature of the conservative form of enjoyment. If no readily apparent enemy exists, the Right will create one.

Enjoying through an enemy is an attempt to disavow the recognition that no one can belong, that everyone doesn't belong collectively. What the Right cannot recognize is that nonbelonging is the source of all enjoyment, even the conservative form. This form of enjoyment enjoys through the nonbelonging that it assigns to the enemy, while believing that there are those who belong and avoid this fate. Right-wing enjoyment wants to have the cake of recognition while eating it too and enjoying the failure of nonrecognition in the enemy. The problem that conservative enjoyment wrestles with is that there is no enjoyment of belonging. The more one tries to fit in, the more one retreats from one's own enjoyment. Whenever and however one enjoys, one is enjoying the fact of nonbelonging, the point of impossibility within the social structure. This is why right-wing enjoyment so obsessively focuses on its enemies in a way that the Left need not do.

The contrast between Right and Left enjoyment is evident in the slogans chanted at rallies during the Trump presidency. At the Unite the Right rally in Charlottesville, Virginia, on August 11, 2017, protesters chanted, "Jews will not replace us," among other racist slogans (including "blood and soil," a revival of the Nazi watchwords *"Blut und Boden"*). This refrain typifies the rightist form of enjoyment. It identifies an enemy that gives the protesters a sense of their own belonging, since it marks a threat to this belonging—the threat of a "replacement."[22] The enemy makes their position of belonging an enjoyable one. They enjoy through those whom they fear will replace them. Without an enemy to chant about, they would not have come to the rally.

The protest against the murder of George Floyd represents a leftist contrast. Demonstrators here did not say, "the police will not replace us" but rather "I can't breathe," the words of the dying George Floyd. The difference between the slogan of Charlottesville and that of Minneapolis (where Floyd's murder took place) encapsulates the difference between rightist and leftist politics. The protesters identified themselves with the figure of nonbelonging who the police killed precisely because they viewed him through the lens of his nonbelonging. For the police, George Floyd did not belong, which is why an officer could crush his throat without any compunction. The leftist movement that arose around Floyd's death focused on this nonbelonging and attempted to reveal its universality, to force those who felt secure in their belonging to see themselves in George Floyd and not in the police officer choking the life out of him. The rallies that took place in the wake of Floyd's murder demonstrated leftist enjoyment: people were protesting an unjust structure by aligning themselves

---

22 Rightists around the Western world invest a great deal of energy in the great replacement theory, the idea that Muslims from the Arab world are in the process of replacing white Christians in Europe and the United States. On FOX News, Tucker Carlson gives voice to this position, as does Éric Zemmour in France. The term first gained popularity when Renaud Camus used it as the title for a book, namely Renaud Camus, *Le Grand Remplacement: Introduction au remplacisme globale* (Plieux: Renaud Camus, 2011).

with the person crushed by it. The enjoyment here didn't require an enemy to attack but occurred through the assertion of universal nonbelonging.

It is absolutely crucial that the emancipatory movement does not militate for universal belonging. There can be no emancipatory attempt to bring those who don't belong within because the sense of belonging cannot be universalized. No matter how many people we include, belonging will always require some who don't belong in order to affirm that others do. In order to gain a sense of belonging, I must be able to see someone else who embodies nonbelonging.[23] If a movement argues for more belonging, we know that it is inherently impossible to universalize and thus inherently conservative in the form of enjoyment it proffers.[24] There is no emancipation of the particular.

---

23 This is the basis for Sigmund Freud's critique of Christianity and Marxism as emancipatory projects. He argues that both political struggles necessitate an enemy in order to secure the belonging of those within these projects. He claims that Marxism "diverts the aggressive tendencies which threaten all human communities to the outside and finds support in the hostility of the poor against the rich and of the hitherto powerless against the former rulers." Sigmund Freud, *New Introductory Lectures on Psycho-Analysis*, trans. James Strachey, *The Standard Edition of the Complete Psychological Works of Sigmund Freud*, ed. James Strachey (London: Hogarth, 1964), 22:180. While Freud's analysis of Stalinism is undoubtedly correct—it did function through the creation of an enemy—he does not envision the possibility of a leftist project that doesn't turn to the Right, that sustains its universality. He fails to see this path because he rejects the idea of politics without an enemy.

24 The marriage equality movement represents an apparent drive for more belonging because it seeks to include more people in the social institution of marriage. This structure, in fact, led several leading queer theorists to oppose the movement, seeing it as a conservative gesture in the direction of the heteronormative society. While it is possible that this interpretation is the correct one, there is a countervailing tendency that the opponents of the movement clearly grasped. Rather than creating more belonging, the marriage equality movement helped to dissolve the belonging associated with marriage. With marriage available to gay couples, it ceases to provide heterosexual couples with the sense of belonging that it once did.

In contrast to the leftist project of universal nonbelonging, the rightist attempt to forge belonging for a particular group always founders on the problem of contradiction that undermines this belonging. No social order can be whole without suffering a point of contradiction where it opens to the outside. No matter how many enemies the Right erects to produce a sense of belonging, this belonging will always be ephemeral and uncertain. The bond of belonging constantly sows the seeds of its own destruction. It requires the very enemy that it aims to destroy. The more successful the conservative project is in doing away with its enemies, the more it eliminates the source of the enjoyment it provides and thereby destroys its own reason for being. This is why every right-wing project is inherently self-defeating, while every left-wing project is inherently tenuous. The Right forges a belonging that depends on those who don't, those whom the Right tries to eliminate, while the Left can't rely on belonging at all. To struggle for emancipation is to find oneself without a group that would give one an identity. Leftism has nothing to hold people together other than their commitment to a shared failure to belong and the enjoyment that this failure provides. The tenuousness of the leftist bond is at once the source of its enjoyment.

2.

From Pleasure
to Enjoyment

GRASPING THE POLITICS OF enjoyment requires recognizing the difference between enjoyment and pleasure. Enjoyment and pleasure exist in a dialectical relationship. Enjoyment is the privileged term in this relationship, as it drives the subject unconsciously. People act for the sake of their enjoyment, even though enjoyment can never become their conscious goal. It is unconscious desire that mobilizes enjoyment, not deliberate planning. Pleasure, on the other hand, is often a person's conscious goal, even if one is not aware of what produces pleasure. Pleasure and enjoyment work dialectically in the following way: by consciously striving for pleasure, a person produces enjoyment, which occurs as an unconscious aim of the conscious attempt to achieve pleasure.

While it may appear as if the distinction between pleasure and enjoyment is a distinction without a difference, just a semantic or a psychoanalytic concern, it actually has clear political consequences. Pleasure occurs within the coordinates of the social field. We can make sense of pleasure. But enjoyment takes place at the point where sense breaks down, where the social field becomes contradictory and no longer accounts for what people experience. The contradictory quality of enjoyment makes it painful to endure, and yet its status as excessive relative to the field of meaning allows it to play a determining role in structuring our existence. Because enjoyment exceeds the realm of signification, it is meaningless. But this structural position allows it to give a direction to what we do in a way that pleasure cannot.

We experience pleasure when we remain within the confines of the social order and acquire an available desired object, whereas enjoyment necessarily occurs at the limit of the structure, at the point where we no longer belong to it. The pleasurable object can be a new job, a romantic partner, a bounty of cash, or even a juicy hamburger. No matter the content of what gives me pleasure, in order to remain just pleasurable, it must also remain within the limits of what my society presents to me as possible. All of these objects fit within the possibilities that the social order makes available to me. None straddle its limits.

Freud defines pleasure in a precise way that initially appears counterintuitive. He sees pleasure obtained through the lessening of a person's excitation rather than through the increase of it. According to his conception of the pleasure principle formulated in the *Introductory Lectures on Psycho-Analysis*, "pleasure is *in some way* connected with the diminution, reduction or extinction of the amounts of stimulus prevailing in the mental apparatus, and that similarly unpleasure is connected with their increase."[1] As he goes on to discuss, the proof that this conception must be right is the sexual act itself. Everything in the act moves toward its culmination in orgasm, which we experience as the greatest pleasure imaginable. Freud continues, "An examination of the most intense pleasure which is accessible to human beings, the pleasure of accomplishing the sexual act, leaves little doubt" about the validity of the pleasure principle.[2] Although the discharge of excitation is more materially evident in the case of men than of women, the

---

1   Sigmund Freud, *Introductory Lectures on Psycho-Analysis*, trans. James Strachey, in *The Complete Psychological Works of Sigmund Freud*, ed. James Strachey (London: Hogarth Press, 1963), 16:356.

2   Sigmund Freud, *Introductory Lectures on Psycho-Analysis*, 16:356.

sexual conduct of both sexes and the intersexed nonetheless supports Freud's theory.[3]

The conclusion of the sexual act is, for almost everyone, the highlight of the process—maybe even the highlight of life itself—because it marks the height of pleasure.[4] When one thinks of it this way, the conception of the pleasure principle as the discharge rather than the accumulation of excitation makes much more sense and ceases to seem counterintuitive. To get rid of excitation is to experience a great, albeit brief, rush of pleasure. Even those blessed with the ability to have multiple orgasms are nonetheless condemned to pleasure's brevity. They simply get to experience this brevity more often than those less gifted.

Pleasure is necessarily momentary because it is a culmination. One experiences pleasure with the diminution of excitation, and then the experience of pleasure is quickly over when there is no more excitation left to diminish. The fleeting nature of pleasure is evident not only in the sexual act but also in the case of eating a Twinkie or a doughnut, which vanishes after a few seconds of pure delight. It even applies to the new BMW that I purchase. The first few times that I drive it, I experience the pleasure of being a Bimmer owner and driver, but this eventually dissipates. Pleasure cannot last. I may later have the pleasure of remembering the earlier experience, but this is a different pleasure, not a continuation of the same one.

---

3 We should not locate any inherent sexism in the concept of the pleasure principle, which is not to say that we should accept it as the final word, especially because Freud himself does not.

4 Even the opponents of psychoanalysis tend to agree with Freud on this point. Michel Foucault fantasized about dying at the moment of orgasm because this is the moment of maximum pleasure. This unusual correlation between the founder of psychoanalysis and its intransigent opponent confirms the commonsensical status of the pleasure principle. It also offers a compelling reason why we should call it into question as the last word on things.

This leads Freud to lament that we are structured psychically so as to be incapable of sustained pleasure. While we might imagine a utopia of constant pleasure, the structure of our psyche makes living in such a utopia impossible. The best that we can hope for is rapid repetition of the pleasurable experience in which we discharge our excess excitation. But every build-up of excitation involves us in unpleasure until we are able to discharge what we have built up, so this utopia would maximize unpleasure just as it maximized pleasure, which many would consider less than utopian.[5]

Freud's theory of pleasure—the pleasure principle—enables him to understand, albeit indirectly, why we give ourselves various difficulties. We do so because putting an end to these difficulties, whatever they might be, brings pleasure. With the concept of the pleasure principle, Freud implicitly explains self-destructiveness by offering his version of the old joke about the man who continually hits himself on the head with a hammer. His friend asks him, "Why are you doing such a patently ridiculous activity?" The man replies, "Because it feels so good when I stop." This good feeling that comes when one stops banging the hammer on one's head is the pleasure of the pleasure principle.

This is how Freud, at the point in his thinking when he writes *The Interpretation of Dreams*, explains unpleasant dreams. As he conceives it, we are not drawn toward negativity as such but simply want to create a path through which we can experience the pleasure of fulfilling a wish. In the book, Freud spends suspiciously little time on bad dreams, given their ubiquity. When he does

---

5 Most utopias follow the reality principle rather than the pleasure principle. For instance, in his *Utopia*, Thomas More minimizes all potential ways of building up excitation: no one wears sexy clothes; no one eats different food than others; no one accumulates wealth; and so on. More's theory, which almost all later utopians follow, is that adhering to the reality principle and keeping excitation to a minimum will produce a more stable and contented society.

address them, he claims, "what is distressing may not be represented in a dream; nothing in our dream-thoughts which is distressing can force an entry into a dream unless it at the same time lends a disguise to the fulfilment of a wish."[6] Although Freud does briefly consider the nightmare in *The Interpretation of Dreams*, it has a necessarily derivative status, due to the prominence of the pleasure principle in that work. The whole point is getting rid of disturbances, not desiring to encounter them.

As long as Freud thinks solely in terms of the opposition between the pleasure principle and its corollary the reality principle (in which one takes into account social restrictions on the path to the release of excitation), there is no possibility for enjoyment, no possibility for an experience that brings the subject satisfaction through the stimulation that it causes for itself rather than through the release of stimulation. This is the position that predominates in Freud's early thinking about how the psyche functions. It leaves him unable to explain why people desire objects that bring them incredible suffering, which is a stubborn fact of the psyche.[7]

Given Freud's conception of the pleasure principle, he explains the building up of excess excitation—in foreplay, for instance—as simply prefatory to the eventual release. One builds up tension or excitation just to give oneself something to discharge. There is no intrinsic value in the excitation itself. Becoming all hot and bothered is only important because it is the prelude to a future release that will be an end to this unpleasant state and

---

6 Sigmund Freud, *The Interpretation of Dreams (Second Part)*, trans. James Strachey, in *The Complete Psychological Works of Sigmund Freud*, ed. James Strachey (London: Hogarth Press, 1953), 5:470–471.

7 Pleasure's brevity enables it to exist unmixed with suffering. One might cry when one's ice cream cone is gone, but this subsequent sadness is distinct from the pleasure that one had while eating it. The absence of any admixture with suffering enables pleasure to seem appealing, but its transience places a fundamental limit on its political valence. Because they are gone so quickly, there are no radical pleasures.

produce pleasure. One must begin by creating the problem that the discharge of excitation through the pleasure principle will solve. The problem has value only insofar as its sequel takes place. But pleasure is only the end of the subject's story. Enjoyment occurs before it reaches this end, which is what Freud will eventually see when he writes *Beyond the Pleasure Principle* in 1920 and conceives of a death drive that thrives on disturbances rather than striving to eliminate them.

The death drive is a contradictory agency. It erects obstacles in its path and gets off on the obstacles rather than on overcoming them. In the death drive, the primacy of the obstacle causes the distinction between suffering and enjoyment to dissipate. One enjoys what thwarts one's conscious wish, what causes one trouble. Whereas pleasure derives from overcoming contradictions, enjoyment occurs within them.

As Freud comes to recognize while writing *Beyond the Pleasure Principle*, we experience pleasure through the diminution of excitation, but we experience enjoyment through creation of it.[8] In contrast to pleasure, we derive enjoyment from what produces a disturbance in our psychic equilibrium. But we cannot simply create excitation by wishing it into existence. The psyche becomes excited through the emergence of a problem. What makes our existence enjoyable is the posing of questions, not the answering of them, the discovery of problems, not their solution, the erection of obstacles, not their elimination.

To put it in psychoanalytic terms, we become excited through the emergence of an object that arouses desire but remains always unattainable. Enjoyment requires a lost or absent object that can never become present and that exists only insofar as it is lost. The

---

8   Although Freud makes the great leap forward of theorizing the death drive, he does not make enjoyment (or *Genuss*) central to his thinking. It falls to Lacan, in his later theorizing, to fill this lacuna when he takes up jouissance as one of his primary points of reference.

enjoyable object is necessarily contradictory: it is enjoyable only insofar as it isn't there. When we enjoy such objects, we enjoy what is not there and take up the contradictory position ourselves. Objects that are just there, objects that are present and not contradictory, have no transcendent value. We can value them as useful objects, but we don't treat them as sublime objects capable of providing enjoyment. Ease of availability indicates that an object is only a quotidian entity. It has no transcendent value but only the status of something to be used.

Transcendent value that goes beyond usefulness emerges through what is absent. The only objects with a transcendent value are those that we cannot access, lost objects. Loss generates excess excitation that leads to enjoyment, which is why the subject must suffer its enjoyment rather than finding pleasure in it. The relationship between enjoyment and loss, a loss that produces excitation and gives the subject something for which to strive, represents the key to the politics of enjoyment.

Let's consider the transformation that an ordinary object undergoes by being lost. I misplace my car keys. Despite looking seemingly everywhere for them, they escape detection. Unlike my phone, I can't call them in order to locate them. The longer I search without being able to find them, the more they become a site for enjoyment, even though under typical circumstances— when I have them at hand—they are the most banal object imaginable. But as they take the form of a lost object while I search for them, I imbue the keys with transcendent enjoyment. They gain a value that goes far beyond just operating my vehicle. Finding them appears to hold the key to all enjoyment, as everything else takes a backseat to the search. But the enjoyment doesn't come from actually finding them. When I do eventually find them, when they become present again as an empirical object, they immediately cease to be the site for enjoyment. I simply feel relief, perhaps a little pleasure. But the enjoyment comes to an end. It consists in the excess excitement that the lost object produces in me that disappears when the object becomes just present.

Enjoyment is always the enjoyment of what isn't there. When an object is constantly present, we find ourselves unable to enjoy it. But when we lose it or it disappears, we experience the object as truly enjoyable. The object's absence animates me. This dynamic is most clearly visible in love relationships. When sex with the partner is an everyday possibility for years, it can turn into a mechanical duty, a duty that many in long relationships opt to forgo. But when one knows that one's time with the partner is limited or when the partner has been away for a long time, the sexual encounter becomes reimbued with enjoyment. Most adages are risible, but the notion that "absence makes the heart grow fonder" does manage to hint at the logic of enjoyment. Because enjoyment involves an engagement with absence, suffering always accompanies it.

Since enjoyment necessarily involves suffering, any attempt to eliminate suffering will meet with intractable resistance. Eliminating suffering is eliminating enjoyment. In order to preserve their possibility for enjoyment, subjects will cling to loss and to the suffering that it entails. Utopian plans for a society organized around the elimination of suffering founder on the requisite role that suffering plays in our enjoyment. If we were to successfully get rid of suffering in a future society, we would simultaneously create an enjoyment-free society. Such a world is not only practically impossible but theoretically impossible as well. Unless utopia contains non-utopian elements, it can have nothing to make it enjoyable for us—and thus there is no way that we can desire to create it.[9] Utopia without non-utopian elements would be something other than utopia.

---

9   What makes Fredric Jameson's recent utopia possible to desire is its obvious deficiency rather than its perfections. In *American Utopia*, Jameson makes the outrageous argument that we should universalize the military and forge

If leftist thinking about the future takes enjoyment into account, it cannot be utopian thinking.[10] An oppressive society, such as contemporary capitalism, strives to keep suffering and enjoyment distinct. This is what makes it oppressive. The social hierarchy and class division depend on those on top enjoying while those below do the suffering. But this distinction can never hold. There is no ability to enjoy while confining all suffering to others. This is the lie of class-based society and the source of the unnecessary suffering that it produces. If one does not suffer one's enjoyment, one misses out on it. This holds for the wealthy as well as for the immiserated, even though the wealthy try to buy their way out of this truth.

Emancipation doesn't entail the elimination of suffering but the elimination of the attempted divorce between suffering and enjoyment. Bringing suffering and enjoyment into proximity would ensure the tearing down of mansions that try to keep suffering out and the creation of an egalitarian form of housing that would permit everyone to experience the interdependence of suffering and enjoyment. A society that highlights the connection between suffering and enjoyment would cease trying to hierarchize their relationship. An equal society would be one in which suffering and enjoyment were evenly distributed. Perhaps the highest paying jobs would be the most revolting, and those who

---

a utopia in this way, since support for the military is so strong and since it already functions like a socialist institution. This argument completely elides the fact that support for the military depends on the nationalistic violence that it perpetuates and that Jameson's utopia would eliminate. But this (fatal) flaw in the utopian vision makes it possible to imagine enjoying the world that Jameson envisions.

10 Walter Davis provides a powerful basis for rejecting utopian thought by recognizing its link to reactionary thinking. He claims, "Utopia is nostalgia projected into the future." Walter Davis, The Ohio State University, private conversation. As Davis recognizes, unconscious conservative nostalgia for a supposedly better past haunts the desire at the heart of the utopian project, even though this project is consciously centered on a different future.

have it easy, like professors and stockbrokers, would work for pennies. According to the leftist position, one must pay the price of one's own enjoyment rather than attempting to slough it off on the less fortunate. A move in this direction would be an emancipatory move. But it requires seeing how enjoyment must trump pleasure.

We can understand the contrast between pleasure and enjoyment by returning to the sexual act. According to Freud's conception of the pleasure principle, the culmination of the act—the discharge of excitation—is all. But once we focus on enjoyment rather than the pleasure principle, this vision of things undergoes a total transformation. Rather than seeing the initial flirting, passionate kissing, and intimate touching as merely preliminary to the main event of orgasm, one could interpret orgasm as the momentary pleasure that puts an end to the enjoyment of these preliminaries. The existence of the orgasm enables our consciousness to accept all the obstacles that intervene leading up to it—the flirting, the inconvenient pieces of clothing that must be removed, the fundamental barrier of the other's desire. These obstacles, not the big finish, produce sexual enjoyment. To understand this reversal is to understand how enjoyment works in contrast to pleasure.

The barriers to the culmination of the sexual act are what make the act enjoyable, but no one, except someone with a perverse orientation, would be able to remain contented with the barriers alone and not take the process to its concluding point. We use the orgasm to smuggle our enjoyment of the obstacles to the sex act past the suspicions of consciousness. Even though he never fully articulates it, this is what Freud's discovery of a drive beyond the pleasure principle implies.[11] The point ceases to be the final orgasm and becomes all the trouble that it takes to get there.

---

11 Freud moves beyond the pleasure principle in 1920 when he writes the eponymous work devoted to this move. See Sigmund Freud, *Beyond the Pleasure Principle*, trans. James Strachey, in *The Standard Edition of the*

If the thrill of orgasm renders the sexual example of enjoyment too difficult to accept, one could think instead of the roller coaster ride at an amusement park (which the sexual act models itself on). The pleasure of the roller coaster occurs during the moments when one speeds down the steep slopes at a breathtaking pace. At these moments, one experiences one's excitation diminishing and feels pleasure. But the enjoyment of the roller coaster takes place elsewhere—as one heads slowly up the ramp to prepare for the burst of pleasure. One finds enjoyment in the build-up of excitation or the encounter with an obstacle (the large hill) that occurs in the slow movement that does not provide pleasure. No one would ride a roller coaster that only went uphill and never provided any pleasure because the psyche must find a way to translate its drive for enjoyment into the consciousness of pleasure. But at the same time, no one would ride a roller coaster that only went downhill and provided nothing but pleasure. The interruption of the pleasure is the only site at which one can enjoy. We cannot just renounce pleasure altogether. If there were no pleasure, there would also be no enjoyment. But pleasure functions as the payoff that the unconscious makes to consciousness in order to slip the suffering that enjoyment requires past the censorship of consciousness.

Suffering is a necessary ingredient in enjoyment, as the anxiety produced in the ride up the hill on the roller coaster illustrates. Enjoyment occurs through some form of self-destruction, which is why it is absolutely irreducible to conscious intention. The self-destructive form of enjoyment necessitates that the drive to enjoy must be unconscious. Although one can consciously strive for pleasure, one cannot consciously strive to enjoy since enjoyment involves suffering and damage to the psyche. To attempt consciously to enjoy would inevitably transform the suffering into

---

Complete Psychological Works of Sigmund Freud, ed. James Strachey (London: Hogarth Press, 1955), 18:1–64.

pleasure, just like trying to throw a game changes loss into a form of victory. If one actually loses the game, one succeeds in throwing it. If one tries consciously to suffer, one succeeds in suffering and perversely turns it into a pleasure. In this sense, because enjoyment requires suffering, because one must suffer one's enjoyment, the pursuit of it must remain unconscious. But the fundamental link to an absent object gives enjoyment its potential political radicality, even if it cannot be the result of conscious planning, which causes problems for integrating enjoyment consciously into political struggles.

But enjoyment has a radicality that pleasure lacks. Pleasures are always recognized pleasures or pleasures of recognition. They occur in places that the social order authorizes, such as the purchase of expensive commodities or the experience of social approbation. Even illegal activity can be socially acceptable and bring pleasure rather than enjoyment. This is what occurs when people shoplift or take kickbacks or cheat on their taxes. These acts violate the law but remain within the realm of what capitalist society recognizes as acceptable because they participate in the demand to accumulate without limits. Anyone who submits to this demand stays on the terrain of capitalist society and its unwritten regulations. Doing so limits one primarily to pleasures.

Enjoyment, in contrast, occurs at a point where recognition no longer holds. Social authorities of whatever stripe never officially sanction enjoyment. Or, as Joan Copjec puts it, "jouissance flourishes only there where it is *not* validated by the Other."[12] That is, there is no social authority that provides the framework through which one enjoys since enjoyment always goes beyond

---

12 Joan Copjec, *Imagine There's No Woman: Ethics and Sublimation* (Cambridge: MIT Press, 2002), 167. Even though enjoyment occurs in a contradictory gap in the structure of signification, it nonetheless relies on the Other in order to form at all. There is no such thing as an isolated enjoyment, an enjoyment that occurs without reference to otherness. Enjoyment breaks down the barrier between self and otherness.

such symbolic frameworks, occurring at the contradictory points of impossibility within them. One enjoys what is absent within the symbolic framework, not what has a place there. Even when enjoyment operates in a conservative fashion, it is nonetheless a potentially radical experience that some force has turned in a conservative direction.

All enjoyment is the enjoyment of nonbelonging. One enjoys the escape from recognition and validation, the freedom from social authorities. Enjoyment is emancipatory because it coincides with the subject's freedom from the constraint of external determinations.[13] The contradiction that inhabits the social order and undermines all authority becomes the source of the subject's enjoyment rather than an external limit. The enjoyment of emancipation occurs through confronting the limit as internal rather than external, through confronting constraint as our own rather than as externally imposed on us.

---

13 The model for free enjoyment is not the ultimate transgression but the Kantian moral law. As Kant conceives it, giving the moral law to ourselves is the only way that we can free ourselves from the determinations that accompany our social situation. The moral law does not derive from this social situation but from our spontaneous self-relation as subjects of signification. It thus opens up a field for acting that has no cause in the situation that otherwise would fully determine us. We enjoy freedom from the dictates of our society by heeding the command that we give ourselves through the moral law. In his own (albeit unspoken) way, Kant theorizes the opposition between pleasure and enjoyment, between the pleasures of following society's rules and the enjoyment of freedom that comes when we obey the moral law.

3.

Called Up to the
Spartacus League

ALTHOUGH ENJOYMENT PLAYS THE decisive role in politics, a struggle exists over what form this enjoyment will take. This struggle can go in many different directions, but its fundamental direction is the alternative between Right and Left, between conservatism and emancipation. Both conservatism and emancipation partake of the same source of enjoyment. After this, however, they mobilize this enjoyment in dramatically different ways. While rightist enjoyment is necessarily tied to a particular group and offers an enjoyment only for this group, leftist enjoyment is universalist. It never confines itself to the particular as the rightist alternative must but is instead open to everyone.

Right-wing enjoyment requires an enemy to serve as a frontier separating those who belong from those who don't. By protecting the particular enjoyment of those who belong from threatening outsiders, the rightist movement actually creates the enjoyment that it protects through the act of protecting it. The enemy is not just a threat but is also—and this is what no right-wing movement can avow—the source of the particular enjoyment. The image of a menacing enemy threatens this enjoyment into existence, just as a car alarm can transform a cheap clunker into a site of enjoyment. By purchasing an alarm for my unappealing car, I convince myself that the car is actually worth stealing, that someone might go to the trouble of taking it. Through this gesture, the formerly worthless car appreciates in value and acquires a value in my eyes that it doesn't really have.

The threat performs a constitutive function for the particular enjoyment of the Right. Nazism in Germany enjoys through the Jew; Fidesz in Hungary enjoys through the immigrant; and so on. The enemy brings about the enjoyment that the enemy threatens as a result of the threat. One can begin to enjoy being a German or being a Hungarian once the threat establishes this identity as imperiled and thus as desirable. Otherwise, there is nothing inherently enjoyable about being a German or a Hungarian. On their own, these identities are just as empty as any others.

Someone is clearly responsible for the problems that occur in the rightist project. There is no right-wing enjoyment without an enemy who threatens it. This form of enjoyment requires the figure of the Jew or some equivalent, be it the immigrant, the racialized other, the Muslim, the Catholic, or someone else. If the Aryan German did not have the figure of the Jew as indicative of what is not German, it would be impossible to enjoy being a German. The Nazi enjoys through the despised figure of the Jew that doesn't belong to German society and acts as a menace to its continued existence.

Even though right-wing enjoyment translates the social contradiction into an opposition with a threatening enemy, it nonetheless continues to find the figure of nonbelonging as the source of enjoyment, just as the Left does. While the Left openly takes up the cause of nonbelonging and privileges this enjoyment, the Right accesses the enjoyment of nonbelonging indirectly by taking those who don't belong as the enemy. It enjoys through the threat that this enemy who doesn't belong poses. The Right's transformation of the radical enjoyment of nonbelonging necessitates that its adherents blind themselves to the source of their enjoyment. No members of the anti-immigrant Alternative für Deutschland can admit to themselves that their enjoyment is that of the immigrant, nor can the followers of Augusto Pinochet in Chile recognize their own enjoyment in that of the socialist enemy. This same structural dynamic characterizes every right-wing movement. To be a rightist means that one is structurally barred from seeing the actual source of one's enjoyment, which is not the case for the Left.

In contrast to the rightist alternative, left-wing enjoyment does not require an enemy. This is crucial to the distinction between Left and Right. Rather than relying on a shared enemy to hate, leftist enjoyment emerges through the bond of a shared nonbelonging. The leftist enjoys through the position of nonbelonging just as the rightist does, with the difference that the leftist identifies itself with this nonbelonging that the rightist views as a threat. What links the Left together is what threatens the Right and bonds the Right together through that threat. From the perspective of emancipation, those who don't belong are not the enemy because nonbelonging is a universal position. As a result of this universalism, the leftist doesn't require an enemy, although it does have adversaries in the form of those who cling to their particularity and reject universality.

This form of enjoyment becomes most evident when a collective identification with someone in the position of the society's enemy occurs. Instead of joining in the ostracism of this figure, those on the side of emancipation identify with the one ostracized. This is how emancipatory enjoyment works. When the oppressive authorities come looking for the enemy to destroy, they no longer find the ostracized minority but a group identified with this figure that gets in the way of any aggressive action. The leftist mantra is "I am Spartacus," a statement of identification not with Spartacus the leader but with Spartacus the target of Roman authorities.[1] Identification with the ostracized is a way of defend-

---

1   According to historical evidence, it appears that the famous line derives from Stanley Kubrick's epic *Spartacus* (1960) rather than from actual events. When the Roman authorities captured Spartacus and his followers after he had led a dramatic slave revolt, they demanded that he identify himself.

ing those ostracized while also affirming an emancipatory form of enjoyment. Through this identification with the ostracized, the leftist becomes excessive and participates in the enjoyment of shared nonbelonging.

One of the most successful forms of shared nonbelonging in human history occurred in Denmark after the Nazi invasion. Rather than acquiescing to or joining in the Nazi assault on the Jews as the other conquered nations in Europe did, Denmark reacted through an emancipatory identification with the Jews as figures of nonbelonging. When the Nazis came looking for the Danish Jews, the Danes in effect proclaimed, "I am Jewish," as a group. Although it is not the case that the Danish people collectively wore the yellow star in an act of solidarity, this myth that they did so does have a foundation in the reality of the radical Danish political act. They hid Jews, smuggled them into neutral Sweden, and generally did whatever they could to thwart Nazi violence against them. When antisemites attacked a synagogue in Copenhagen, the Danish authorities punished them with the full force of the law.

In October 1943, Germany issued a deportation order for Danish Jews, but the Danish resistance successfully smuggled the vast majority of the Jews into hiding or out of the country. As a result, only a little over one hundred of the approximately 7,800 Jews in Denmark perished in the Holocaust. As Hannah Arendt points out, "The story of the Danish Jews is *sui generis*, and the behavior of the Danish people and their government was unique among all the countries of Europe—whether occupied, a partner of the Axis, or neutral and truly independent. One is tempted to recommend the story as required reading in political science for

---

Before he could do so, several of his followers proclaimed themselves to be him. This is the model for leftist enjoyment, which is why if this assertion of emancipatory universality did not actually occur, Kubrick was certainly correct to invent it.

all students who wish to learn something about the enormous power potential inherent in non-violent action and resistance to an opponent possessing vastly superior means of violence."[2] The miracle of the Danish response to Nazism does not just consist in its nonviolent resistance to violence but in the form of enjoyment that it depicts. It represents a paradigmatic act of emancipatory enjoyment that doesn't rely on an enemy but actively seeks to bring the enemy over to the side of collective nonbelonging.

Even if the figure of the fascist or the capitalist is an opponent of the leftist project, this figure is not an enemy to be eliminated. This is why the Danish resistance was able to convert several German soldiers to their position, to persuade them to abandon the pursuit of Jews to be sent to death camps.[3] The political courage that the Danes showed in the face of Nazi aggression was the courage of universal nonbelonging, which made it readily available to the Germans they were fighting. Some Germans recognized themselves in the universality of the Danish cause and thus came to view their own cause as too particular. They looked on themselves from the perspective of the universal and found their own position wanting.

A similar dynamic appeared in the Black Lives Matter protests of 2020. On several occasions, protesters asked the police against whose actions they were protesting to join them in their

---

2   Hannah Arendt, *Eichmann in Jerusalem: A Report on the Banality of Evil* (New York: Penguin, 2006), 171.

3   Arendt comments on the effect that the Danish resistance had on some Germans. She writes, "It is the only case we know of in which the Nazis met with *open* native resistance, and the result seems to have been that those exposed to it changed their minds. They themselves apparently no longer looked upon the extermination of a whole people as a matter of course. They had met resistance based on principle, and their 'toughness' had melted like butter in the sun, they had even been able to show a few timid beginnings of genuine courage." Hannah Arendt, *Eichmann in Jerusalem*, 175. Such conversion is only possible because emancipatory enjoyment does not function as a closed set.

political act. This was only possible because the protesters viewed the police as adversaries rather than as enemies and because their position was universalist. Although only a few officers availed themselves of this opportunity, the fact that some did, the fact that some knelt with the protesters, indicates the universality of the emancipatory project and proves that Black Lives Matter was not a case of identity politics. Such an act would be impossible to imagine in a rightist movement, since such movements are inherently particularist and rely on an enemy that cannot be brought into the fold. One cannot chant "Jews will not replace us" and simultaneously invite Jews to join in. The enemy must remain external and can never be simply an adversary.

If a rightist movement such as the Alternative für Deutschland in Germany or the Rassemblement National in France decided to open its arms to its enemy, the immigrant, this would destroy the coherence of the movement. These movements depend on the enemy remaining outside and not becoming part of the movement. They constitute enjoyment for their members only as long as the figure of nonbelonging—the immigrant, in this case—is in the position of the threat. Without a threat, the enjoyment would dissipate, and the movement would dry up. To admit enemies into the movement necessitates its transformation into a universalist struggle for emancipation, which would entail the abandonment of the anti-immigrant platform that defines the movement. The rightist movement promises belonging, which requires the image of someone that doesn't belong.

The openness to the adversary is only possible insofar as leftism recognizes that the space of belonging is constitutively empty. Emancipatory nonbelonging cannot even target those who appear to belong as the enemy because emancipation has its basis in the universality of nonbelonging. There is no enemy to destroy because there is no one who actually belongs. This is where the emancipatory project has an advantage over the rightist one.

Rightism must create a sense of belonging that can never become secure because belonging is always just an illusion that depends on those who threaten it. If the truth of universal nonbelonging becomes apparent, the right-wing movement will collapse. All belonging is just the failure to recognize the universality of non-belonging, which is what every genuine leftist program insists on.

As a result of its absence of enemies, the leftist project privileges forgiveness of those who position themselves as adversaries of universal equality and insist on the priority of their particular identity. One can always forgive a former adversary, whereas an enemy is unpardonable. The project of emancipation is always ready to welcome former adversaries into its ranks while offering expiation for past transgressions of universality. This willingness to forgive derives from the openness of the emancipatory project. Because it offers no identity to which one might belong, participation in emancipation is open to all, even those who had formerly been the opponents of equality.

4.

Anticommunists
or Monks

THE CONTRAST BETWEEN RIGHTIST and leftist enjoyment is evident in the arena of comedy, although perhaps not in the way that one might initially think. It is not the case that leftists are always funny and rightists lack a sense of humor, or even that rightists are funny and politically correct leftists can never joke. Things aren't so clear cut. However, there is a basic political distinction operating in comedy. The right-wing joke operates according to a strict opposition between belonging and nonbelonging, just as right-wing enjoyment does. This type of joke identifies a contradiction within the enemy who doesn't belong and finds the humor in it, but it leaves the friend in a position of wholeness, free of any evident contradiction. A joke is not conservative, contrary to contemporary popular opinion, simply because it punches down.[1] The conservative dimension of the right-wing joke does not derive from whom it targets but from whom it insulates from contradiction. Right-wing comedy has those who belong that it refuses to make fun of. A genuine leftist comedy accepts no such restrictions but sees the comedy of contradiction everywhere.

The right-wing structure becomes apparent in almost any anticommunist joke. A standard one goes like this: What is the best way to kill communists? The answer: Communism. This joke is

---

1   Many comic acts in Charlie Chaplin's films involve punching down, and yet his comedy is wholly aligned with the Left because he refuses to leave anyone safe from comic contradiction.

funny. It correctly apprehends the self-destructive manifestations of actual communist experiments in the twentieth century, but it's a right-wing joke because it postulates the communist as the enemy that succumbs to a contradiction that leaves the anticommunist intact. Although the joke apprehends how communism undermines itself (or has done so historically), it leaves the anticommunist undivided and positions communism in the position of the enemy to be annihilated. We know that this is a right-wing joke because it preserves the anticommunist position as a position free from any contradiction.

Rightist enjoyment confines itself to those who belong—to those who aren't communists, in the example of the right-wing anticommunist joke. While communists in the joke suffer from contradiction, the anticommunist telling the joke does not. The anticommunist enjoys through the contradiction that undermines communism while insulating the anticommunist position itself from contradiction. The anticommunist belongs while the communist doesn't, and the nonbelonging of the communist ensures the belonging of the anticommunist.

This form of enjoyment is necessarily particular and cannot accede to the universal. If it were to become universal, it would lose the exclusivity that gives it its right-wing hue. Through the insistence on belonging, rightist enjoyment depends on the enemy that its jokes turn into a source of mockery, a mockery that correctly identifies the lack in the enemy but that leaves the friend unstained with contradiction. Leftism, in contrast, finds enjoyment within its own contradiction. This enjoyment is universal because contradiction inheres in every identity.

The fundamental contradiction that animates leftist politics is its insistence of universal nonbelonging that leaves the position of belonging empty. Structurally, there is a position of belonging, but no one can occupy this position. This dynamic is inherently humorous and lends itself to jokes. Let's look at a joke that captures the articulation of contradiction as a site for enjoyment. A visitor arrives at a monastery to investigate what life is like there. One of the monks agrees to act as his guide and to explain their idiosyncratic ways. When dinnertime comes, the monk takes the visitor to a large dining hall. As they start to eat, a random monk screams out, "Fifteen," and the hall erupts with laughter. The visitor is perplexed and wonders about this bizarre ritual. He asks his guide for an explanation. The guide tells him, "We have all been together so long that we know all the jokes that everyone tells, so rather than going through the trouble of explaining a whole joke, we just use the shortcut of a number. Just after this explanation, another monk yells out, "Fifty-six." This time the laughter is more subdued. The visitor enquires about this change. His guide says, "It's simple. That joke just wasn't as funny as the first." By this time, the visitor thinks he has the hang of it and wants to try his hand at telling a joke. He shouts, "One hundred and twenty-five." The dining hall explodes in more laughter than even the first joke provoked. The visitor says to the guide, "Wow, I must have told a really funny one." The guide responds, "Well, we hadn't heard that one before." What's fascinating about this joke is that it recounts laughter occurring at an empty space: everyone laughs at a joke that no one knows. The joke allows the listener to join in the laughter at a joke that doesn't exist.

The monastery joke provides the perfect paradigm for leftist enjoyment because there is no one who knows the joke that provokes laughter in everyone. The group that belongs—those who know the joke—is empty. Everyone laughs, but no one knows the joke that they are collectively laughing at. No one belongs, although there is a universal nonbelonging. Even the monks who have lived their whole lives at the monastery inhabit the position of nonbelonging in the joke because they know no more than the visitor. This nonbelonging is not, however, a new form of belonging precisely because there is no one excluded from it. It is a nonbelonging that doesn't require anyone to oppose itself to but rather uses belonging as a formal position with which to distinguish its universality. The enjoyment in the monastery joke doesn't depend on anyone in the position of the enemy. The adversary is a form, not a content, an absence rather than an identifiable enemy.

The Left enjoys what is not there—like the joke that the visitor to the monastery tells. The nonexistence of this joke that corresponds to the number he yells out is the joke itself. We laugh together at the impossible position that the joke itself occupies and the contradiction that this implies. In leftist comedy, there is no position immune to the reach of contradiction. Leftism is the enjoyment of contradiction—the point at which the symbolic structure ceases to hold. Because contradiction extends everywhere, this enjoyment is not exclusive. No one need be barred from it for someone to experience it. Some don't suffer so that others can enjoy.[2] All suffer so that no one is excluded from enjoyment.[3]

The contrast between the anticommunist joke and the monastery joke makes visible the difference between Right and Left. As the contrast between these jokes suggests, Right and Left are not so much opposed ways of looking at the world as opposed structures of enjoyment. If right-wing political activity has an inherent advantage over leftism, it consists in the facility with which the Right can structure a path to enjoyment. It is always easy to

---

2   The structure that forces many to suffer so that others can enjoy on the basis of their suffering is the logic of slavery, as Sheldon George describes it. According to George, within the logic of slavery, "the white subject's *jouissance* becomes the instrument of African Americans' confrontation with trauma." Sheldon George, *Trauma and Race: A Lacanian Study of African American Racial Identity* (Waco, TX: Baylor University Press, 2016), 8.

3   To put it in the terms of the science fiction masterpiece *In Time* (Andrew Niccol, 2011), "No one should be immortal, if even one person has to die." When Will Salas (Justin Timberlake) says this, he articulates a challenge to a social order that condemns the majority to early death so that the elite few can live for an unlimited amount of time.

identify an enemy, while it is much more difficult to recognize absence as the source of enjoyment.

Rightist enjoyment not only has an enemy; it also has a content. This contrasts with the formal structure of leftist enjoyment. For the Left, the site of enjoyment is bereft of any content, and emancipation depends on sustaining the site of belonging as a field of absence. The moment belonging acquires a content, leftist enjoyment takes on an enemy, which makes it indistinguishable from right-wing enjoyment. When the Left erects an enemy and fills in the absent field of belonging, we can be sure that it has betrayed the difficulty of its form of enjoyment for the ease of the right-wing alternative with its identifiable content.

A leftist organization of society would have to follow the paradigm of the monastery joke. It would have to translate the logic of this joke to the society's political structure, capturing the centrality of nonbelonging that the jokes stresses. Since the historical models for leftist social organization are always fleeting—brief periods in the French and Haitian Revolutions, for example—the joke provides the best and more durable paradigm to examine. It sketches an institutional structure that would form around an empty site of belonging. This is what rightist enjoyment cannot tolerate.

5.

Robespierre
vs. Napoleon

THE CONTRAST BETWEEN RIGHT and Left enjoyment becomes especially evident during the French Revolution. When the forces of the French Revolution propose the values of *liberté, égalité,* and *fraternité* against the monarchical rule of Louis XVI, they propose a form of emancipatory enjoyment that had no clear antecedents in human history.[1] This political program was an assertion of the rights of those who had no stake in French society. The Revolution attempted to grant the figures of nonbelonging a position within the social order. This is why the *sans-culottes* played such a prominent role in the revolutionary struggle. These were the commoners that had no class status—evident in the lack of proper pants that gave them their nom de guerre—and yet articulated demands that at times directed the tide of the revolution. Ultimately, the Revolution devolved into a rightist military coup, but there were moments when it adhered to the process of emancipation.[2] Even

---

1   The enjoyment proffered by the American Revolution was not a predecessor of that at work in the French Revolution. Despite the language of the Declaration of Independence, the American project relied on the nonbelonging of slaves, who had no access to the values it proclaimed. The American Revolution was a particularist, not a universalist, movement.

2   According to legend, we owe the terms *Right* and *Left* as political names to the epoch of the French Revolution. In 1789, the more conservative members of the National Assembly were seated to the right of the monarch, while the advocates of emancipation were seated to the left. Marcel Gauchet shows that, in actuality, the primary division in the National Assembly was vertical

though this movement did not take emancipation to its end point, it marked the most significant emancipatory step that had ever occurred in human history.[3]

Aristocratic rule—the regime in France throughout the Middle Ages—endured because it convinced the majority of the population that the enjoyment that their suffering would bring was an ultimate enjoyment in the afterlife. Enjoyment for almost everyone in Medieval Europe was deferred until later. This is why the Church played such an outsized role in the social order. The Church regulated the relationship between suffering and enjoyment: the more one suffered, the more one would enjoy in the end. But as modernity brought forth a different mode of enjoying—the possibility of not deferring enjoyment—the power of the aristocracy and Church dramatically diminished.

Revolutionary change occurs for a variety of reasons. But one of the most significant is that a form of enjoyment ceases to be acceptable for a large portion of the society. The moment that the social order ceases to deliver enjoyment to a wide enough swath of people is the moment when it becomes vulnerable to revolutionary upheaval. Without any stake in the ruling distribution of enjoyment, one can revolt with impunity. At this point, one has nothing to lose but one's life, and one's life has value only insofar as it leads to at least some modicum of enjoyment. A completely unenjoyable life—one in which suffering doesn't even produce enjoyment—cannot endure because one who doesn't enjoy at all will just put an end to things. The society that fails to provide

---

rather than horizontal, a divide between the Montagnards (Mountain) and the Plaine (Plain) or Marais (Marsh). See Marcel Gauchet, *La droite et la gauche: Histoire et destin* (Paris: Gallimard, 2021). But what the legend nicely illustrates is the contingent origin of the terms *Left* and *Right*, a contingency that enables us to constantly redefine their significance. That is largely what this project is attempting to do.

3   The unparalleled radicality of the French Revolution is what led Hegel to drink a toast to it every July 14th from his teen years until his death.

avenues for enjoyment for the mass of people gives them no reason not to revolt. This situation becomes especially propitious for a revolution when those deprived of enjoyment constantly see others awash in it, as was the case in prerevolutionary France.

From the beginning of the Revolution, those who didn't belong in French society began to assert their value. This is clear in the famous pamphlet from Emmanuel Joseph Sieyès entitled *What Is the Third Estate?* The definition of the third estate was a vital question for the Revolution because it included the people who had no privileges in prerevolutionary French society. The third estate was made up of the commoners who didn't belong. Or, to put it paradoxically, belonging to the third estate was a sign that one didn't belong to prerevolutionary French society. Even though Sieyès was far from being a revolutionary radical—he later joined a government with Napoleon—he nonetheless insisted that France must address itself to the people who don't belong. The claim for the rights of the Third Estate was a claim for the rights of those who didn't belong.

The beginning of *What Is the Third Estate?* lays out the problem of a society where the majority of the people count for nothing. Sieyès states, "1. What is the Third Estate?—Everything. 2. What, until now, has it been in the existing political order?—Nothing. 3. What does it want to be?—Something."[4] With this statement, the case is clear: the commoners do the work, but they don't enjoy the fruits of their labor. The fact that their enjoyment doesn't figure in the social order is the cause for their revolt. The solution that Sieyès proposes—that the Third Estate become "something"—reflects his insufficient commitment to revolutionary change and to an emancipatory structure of enjoyment. While Sieyès imagines the common people receiving something, he cannot envision a form of society in which access to enjoyment

---

4   Emmanuel Joseph Sieyès, *What Is the Third Estate?*, trans. Michael Sonenscher, in *Political Writings* (Indianapolis: Hackett, 2003), 94.

would be equally distributed through a recognition of shared nonbelonging, although this is the aim of the Montagnards (the radical members of the National Convention, whose name, "the Mountain," derived from their position sitting high in the legislative chamber) and the other more radical groups participating in the Revolution.

The insistence on liberty, equality, and solidarity is an implicit demand for a new form of enjoyment that ceases to privilege those who have over those who don't—and that ultimately would require an equal distribution of wealth. Nonbelonging asserts its right in the French Revolution, most powerfully through the Montagnards. This revolutionary shift in the site of the society's enjoyment leads the most radical participants to turn away from devotion to the monarch and to instead commit themselves to the people who most conspicuously don't belong. This is the case with Jean-Paul Marat, who published the newspaper *L'Ami du peuple* to express this alignment.

Marat denounced those in the Revolution who remained loyal to the monarch and to the privileges of wealth. He did so in a way that argued for a different form of enjoyment, an enjoyment of those who didn't belong. The vehemence of his attacks forced him to go into hiding in order to evade arrest and even death from those in power. Eventually, an aristocrat hostile to the Montagnards and sympathetic to the more moderate Girondins, Charlotte Corday, killed Marat to silence his radical voice. The assertion of the right of those who don't belong poses such a threat to those invested in their belonging that they often resort to intrigue and murder to protect their position.[5]

---

5   Marat has few champions today, but among those who unequivocally take up his defense is Nadir Lahiji. Lahiji claims that Corday justified her assassination of Marat with lies about him, just as "he was constantly attacked for his newspaper and falsely accused of having a hand in the September massacre." Nadir Lahiji, *Architecture or Revolution: Emancipatory Critique After Marx* (New York: Routledge, 2021), 57. Lahiji sees Marat as the most

One indication of Marat's investment in a new form of enjoyment was his refusal to take the civic oath [*serment civique*] in which one had to pledge fidelity to the king. In an article entitled "The Real Civic Oath" [*"Le Véritable serment civique"*], he clarifies his opposed conception of duty. He states, "I swear to never sacrifice the rights of the people to the guardians of authority and to die of hunger rather than sell their interests."[6] Marat's insistence on an egalitarian social order placed him firmly on the side of the people against the aristocratic monopoly on the society's form of enjoyment, which made the title of his newspaper, *L'Ami du peuple*, appropriate. Marat and his fellow radicals pushed the Revolution to tear down all social privilege, including that of the monarch himself, whom the Revolution eventually executed after his acts of treason.[7] The Revolution upheld the values of *liberté*, égalité, and *fraternité* as an expression of the position of nonbelonging. Initially, it did not require an enemy but fought to establish a republic of nonbelonging.

Because they proffered an enjoyment that didn't rely on exclusion but on universal nonbelonging, the radical participants in the French Revolution insisted that slavery in the colonies, despite the wealth that it brought to France, was incompatible with the new form of enjoyment. The Montagnards saw the basic contradiction involved in the continuation of slavery and the establishment of a republic based on liberty, equality, and solidarity. In a speech to the National Convention in 1791, Maximilien Robespierre made clear that the liberty of the French people depended on *not* continuing to endorse slavery in the colonies. As long as the colonies existed,

---

radical edge of the Revolution, which he calls the defining political event of modernity.

6 Jean-Paul Marat, "Le Véritable serment civique," *Oeuvres de Jean-Paul Marat* (Paris: Décembre-Alonnier, 1869), 161.

7 Whatever one thinks about the death penalty—I'm completely against it— it's nonetheless evident that Louis XVI was guilty of conspiring treasonously with other European governments in order to bring about the downfall of the Revolution in France.

according to Robespierre, there was no way to enjoy freedom in France. He stated, "the supreme interest of the nation and of the colonies themselves is that you would remain free, and that you would not overthrow the bases of this liberty with your own very hands. Death to the colonies."[8] Robespierre's proclamation drew a mixed response in the chamber of the National Convention, but under Jacobin rule, France did end slavery in the colonies. The form of enjoyment that the radical wing of the Revolution tried to introduce was a form without hierarchy, an enjoyment founded in the position of nonbelonging.

As Marat and Robespierre both feared, war proved the downfall of the Revolution. Success in wars against other European nations brought Napoleon Bonaparte great popularity and enabled him to put an end to the Revolution. But it was the failure of the French Revolution to constitute a universalist egalitarian enjoyment that gave Napoleon the space in which he could overthrow its institutions. When Robespierre took up a leading position in the revolutionary government, he spent too much time identifying enemies rather than trying to universalize nonbelonging. He participated in the execution not only of the more moderate Girondins but also of his radical friend Camille Desmoulins and fellow Montagnard Georges Danton. Robespierre turned away from universality to the fabrication of enemies, which included, shockingly, a change of position on both the death penalty and on foreign wars. This rightward turn led not only to his own execution but also to Napoleon's rise, which the revolutionary government's commitment to war made possible.[9] Robespierre himself support-

---

8   Maximilien Robespierre, *Oeuvres de Maximilien Robespierre, Tome VII: Discours Janvier-Septembre 1791*, 362.

9   Even though Robespierre himself turned away from a leftist form of enjoyment, his death marked the end of the emancipatory possibility. With his demise, the society of universal nonbelonging dies out. As Jean-Clément Martin points out, "By killing Robespierre, Thermidor turns the page of heroic mobilization and of emotion considered as the essential link of a community

ed Napoleon as a general, although he was long dead by the time Napoleon came to power. Just as the Revolution itself took advantage of the lack of enjoyment that the monarchy provided for the people, Napoleon capitalized on the inability to envision a form of enjoyment commensurate with the Revolution's own aspirations in order to take power for himself.

In the coup d'état of November 9–10, 1799, Napoleon replaced the democratic Directory with a Consulate that he led. His rule brought a new form of enjoyment that countered that of the Revolution. Although he fought against royalists desiring to restore the monarchy, Napoleon did reinstate the rightist form of enjoyment associated with the monarchy, which is why his rule constantly required an enemy to fight. Under his leadership, France was almost always at war with other European nations. In addition—and unsurprisingly—Napoleon attempted to reintroduce slavery in Haiti by sending the military there.[10] He also introduced the Napoleonic Code into law on March 21, 1804, which took back the egalitarian promise of the French Revolution. It focused on property rights and even made wives into the property of their husbands. The revolutionary concern for the Third Estate ceased to play any role in this new legal structure. But Napoleon's rise allowed the French people to enjoy through his person and his victories. His military gains made possible a nationalist enjoyment that trumped the egalitarian enjoyment of the

---

in order to allow the country to enter into a desacralized politics, consecrated to tangible economic progress." Jean-Clément Martin, *Robespierre: La fabrication d'un monstre* (Paris: Perrin, 2016), 365. The Thermidorian reaction permitted France to enter unequivocally into the capitalist universe.

10 Napoleon's effort to reintroduce slavery in Haiti ultimately failed, but his intervention nonetheless forced Haiti to pay reparations to France for over a hundred years, well into the twentieth century. Rather than paying the former slaves in Haiti reparations for their years of suffering under the yoke of slavery, France, under Napoleon's rule, demanded that the emancipated slaves pay for their freedom.

Revolution. Under Napoleon, one could belong to French society again through his military triumphs and through the empire he established. The enjoyment of nonbelonging drained away just like Marat's blood after Charlotte Corday stabbed him. Enjoyment of the nation always works against that of emancipation, which is why war is an inherently conservative phenomenon, even if waged on behalf of extending revolution to all of Europe.

The trajectory of the French Revolution—from aristocratic to egalitarian to nationalist forms of enjoyment—reveals what's at stake in political struggle. Every political fight involves a battle between competing forms of enjoyment. These forms of enjoyment undergird the various assertions of rights, duties, and responsibilities, and yet, no one can directly assert the importance of enjoyment or the role that it plays. Leaders, whether democratic or autocratic, offer people a vehicle through which they can structure their enjoyment. This is how they relate to their followers. But a form of enjoyment is never simply imposed by a leader. People demand a leader who outlines the vehicle for enjoyment that they find most appealing or on their own collectively opt for a system that appears able to best deliver enjoyment. If a leader doesn't provide an appealing path to enjoyment, people will find one who will.[11] Enjoyment, which goes beyond pleasure and even goes so far as to provide a reason for living, determines why we act in the ways that we do, inclusive of the realm of politics, even if no political actor can ever chart a direct path to it. To understand political struggle as the struggle for a form of enjoyment is to challenge the traditional ways that politics has been understood.

---

11 In *The Wretched of the Earth*, Frantz Fanon insists on conceiving the leader as the result of a collective drive rather than as the driver of social change. He writes, "If the leader drives me I want him to know that at the same time I am driving him. The nation should not be an affair run by a big boss." Frantz Fanon, *The Wretched of the Earth*, 127.

6.

The Power
of the Good

TRADITIONAL DEFINITIONS OF POLITICS locate its determining factor in an idea of the good, not in the assertion of a form of enjoyment. According to this thinking, people construct the society in the best way possible in order to secure the best life they can forge for themselves or for the social order as a whole. Enjoyment, in contrast, is not aligned with prosperity and arrives at the expense of the good rather than through its achievement. Enjoyment requires sacrificing the good, which would not make any sense at all to thinkers who consider the good as the basis of every society.

This perspective that sees the good as the focus of politics is clearest in the case of Aristotle. His philosophy theorizes politics as the art of creating a good society. He begins the *Politics* by claiming, "Every state is a community of some kind, and every community is established with a view to some good; for everyone always acts in order to obtain that which they think good."[1] As this statement reveals, Aristotle extrapolates from individuals' pursuit of what is best for them to the state's pursuit of the good. The idea

---

1   Aristotle, *Politics*, trans. B. Jowett, in *The Complete Works of Aristotle*, vol. 2, ed. Jonathan Barnes (Princeton: Princeton University Press, 1984), 1:1. For his part, John Locke contends, "The end of Government is the good of Mankind." John Locke, *Two Treatises of Government* (New York: Cambridge University Press, 1988), 417. At this closing point of the famous *Second Treatise of Government*, Locke uses the pursuit of the good as the basis for an argument against tyrannical authority, which has the effect of impairing this pursuit.

that a society aims at realizing the good seems straightforward-ly the case. It seems commonsensical that a society is structured around its good rather than around what would undermine it. Many subsequent thinkers agree and follow Aristotle in this line of thinking.[2] For them, the good that a society pursues is not nec-essarily the good of all. It can be, as Aristotle sees it, the good of the few or even the one in the case of a tyrannical rule. No matter how circumscribed it is, the good must act as the political ideal.

Taking Aristotle's philosophy as our point of departure, we could interpret the Iranian Revolution as a conflict between two distinct ideas of the good. The ruling Shah saw the good in the Westernization of Iranian society and its connection to Europe and the United States. His own enrichment certainly also fig-ured in his conception of the good. The Islamicist revolution that brought Ayatollah Ruhollah Khomeini to power organized the good of Iranian society in a completely opposed way. The form of the good that the revolution promoted placed Islam at the center of the society and attempted to eliminate the secularism that it associated with the West. Despite the violent opposition at work, Aristotle would nonetheless see the determining role of the good even in this instance. One could theorize the political opposition at play in terms of opposing conceptions of the good without abandoning the good as the fundamental stake of political con-testation. When considering the good, the question of enjoyment takes a backseat, if it ever emerges at all.

The problem with this emphasis on the good as the driv-ing force of politics is that it runs directly into the wanton

---

2   For instance, despite the dramatic differences between them, both Hannah Ar-endt and John Rawls accept Aristotle's notion that the good is what ultimately matters in politics. This position is what leads Arendt to take up the minority position of preferring the American Revolution to the French. For Arendt, the American Revolution manages to institute the good, whereas the French Revolution simply fails to do so. For a convincing rejoinder to this claim, see Jean-Claude Milner, *Relire la Révolution* (Paris: Éditions Verdier, 2016).

destructiveness of so many societies, a destructiveness that more often than not engulfs not just the enemy but the society itself. This is apparent in many of the horrors of the twentieth century, from Stalin's show trials to Hitler's death camps to Pol Pot's killing fields. These events reflect a destructiveness that doesn't advance the good even of those perpetuating the violence. Hitler's murder of six million Jews eliminated a labor source that might have aided Germany's war effort. Stalin's show trials destroyed many of his best allies, such as Nikolai Bukharin. Pol Pot deprived Cambodia of the intellectuals who could have built a thriving society. In these instances and countless others, self-destructiveness was not just a side effect of the pursuit of the good that these movements undertook but central to their structure, which shows that the good didn't necessarily play a determinative role in these political movements. Both Nazism and Stalinism made obvious their marginalization of the good and made it difficult for theorists of politics to continue to adhere to Aristotle's political philosophy.

We don't have to restrict ourselves to the most obvious horrors of the twentieth century to see how the social order marginalizes the good for the sake of senseless destruction. Capitalist society functions through the production and consumption of excess. It reproduces itself by producing too much and causing the social order to suffocate on its excesses. Crises of overproduction constantly arise in the capitalist epoch because the system can sustain itself only through producing more than enough for a good society. Excess trumps the good in capitalist society, showing that Aristotle must certainly be wrong about the nature of the social order.

Although there are some thinkers who continue even today to theorize in the way that Aristotle does about politics, conceiving politics in terms of the good came to appear much too idealistic for the most influential modern political philosophers. The seemingly mindless destructiveness of modernity prompted the leading political thinkers to consider a dramatically different type of explanation. Inspired by Friedrich Nietzsche, they turned to power as the explanation for why people seek to rule and for how they rule. Nietzsche conceives of the will to power as the driving force that dominates all human existence. For him, the good doesn't orient our political activity but serves as an alibi for the discharge of power that people seek within political struggle.

As Nietzsche conceives it, no one chases after the good but instead works to experience an increase in power. Power even trumps the desire to survive. In *Beyond Good and Evil*, the distinction between the good and power as forms of explanation becomes clearest. Distinguishing power from the good of survival, Nietzsche writes, "Physiologists should think twice before positioning the drive for self-preservation as the cardinal drive of an organic being. Above all, a living thing wants to *discharge* its strength—life itself is will to power—: self-preservation is only one of the indirect and most frequent *consequences* of this."[3] Even though Nietzsche rarely talks about political questions and advances no developed political theory, his emphasis on power as the ultimate explanatory matrix has shaped the discussion in his wake. Across the political spectrum, power has become the most commonly accepted framework for thinking about political struggle.[4] According to this view, the terrain of politics is the terrain where different actors assert their claims to power. Even if they couch their power grab in terms of

---

3   Friedrich Nietzsche, *Beyond Good and Evil: Prelude to a Philosophy of the Future*, trans. Judith Norman (Cambridge: Cambridge University Press, 2002), 15.

4   Judith Butler conceives of power as both what makes us who we are and what we must contest in order to assert who we are. In *The Psychic Life of Power*, she writes, "power is not simply what we oppose but also, in a strong sense, what we depend on for our existence and what we harbor and preserve in the beings that we are." Judith Butler, *The Psychic Life of Power* (Stanford: Stanford University Press, 1997), 2. Power's role in constituting us as subjects complexifies our relation to it, so that one cannot simply oppose oneself to those in power but must realize one's dependence on power as well.

the public good, power acts as the motivating force for what everyone does on the political scene.

Despite Nietzsche's entrenched political conservatism that borders on reactionary thinking, his most important inheritors have been leftists.[5] From Gilles Deleuze and Michel Foucault to Judith Butler and Giorgio Agamben, figures on the Left have seen in Nietzsche's turn to power a way of approaching politics without the naïveté of earlier theorists. Unlike the champions of the good, Nietzsche seems to look unblinkered at the brutal domination occurring throughout the political landscape. But in contrast to Nietzsche himself, these left-leaning followers have used the emphasis on power as a way of criticizing those exercising power over others. In a way that would have appalled Nietzsche himself, the leftist Nietzscheans focus so singularly on power because they find power to be anathema. Their aim is to eliminate the power imbalances that cause oppression in the world, whereas Nietzsche celebrates the fecundity of such imbalances and rues their disappearance in modernity.

Interpreting politics in terms of power is not just in vogue among political philosophers. It has almost reached the status of common sense in the society at large. Power relations come up in casual conversations and public discussions. Nietzsche's claim to a revolutionary interpretation of morality as self-assertion rather than quest for the good would not strike most people today as outrageous in the way that it did many of his contemporaries.

---

5   The leftist appropriation of Nietzsche began in the second half of the twentieth century and continues to this day. Right-wing investment in Nietzsche's thought has become muted after the fall of Nazism, which, despite an open embrace of Nietzsche, was based so clearly on a distortion of his philosophy. In the effort to distance Nietzsche from the Nazi celebration of him, leftist thinkers, beginning with Albert Camus, have pushed him so far that he has more or less ceased to be an attractive thinker for rightist movements, although his thought announces an aristocratic opposition to the movement for equality.

Nietzsche, however, sees a power imbalance as natural and inevitable, whereas most people today understand imbalances in power as inherently immoral.

It is Michel Foucault who plays the primary role in enacting this moralization of Nietzsche's thought. Foucault casts the longest shadow over contemporary thinking about power in politics. As he puts it in an interview, "Power is no longer substantially identified with an individual who possesses or exercises it by right of birth; it becomes a machinery that no one owns. Certainly everyone doesn't occupy the same position; certain positions preponderate and permit an effect of supremacy to be produced."[6] This supremacy is what Foucault and most theorists of power struggle against. Their implicit ideal is a world in which all have power over themselves and no one has power over others. Thus, despite Nietzsche's initial turn to power to move away from the good, the theorists of power smuggle the good back into the political equation, as is clear from Foucault's statement and from similar statements by Judith Butler, Giorgio Agamben, and many others.

This return to the good following the turn to power reveals that power and the good are not as opposed as they initially appear to be. The seemingly revolutionary turn away from the good and toward power actually leaves the good almost entirely intact. It is a revolution in name only because both the good and power operate as ways of protecting ourselves from the disruptiveness of our own enjoyment. The good and power come together as defenses against the threat that enjoyment poses to social stability.

The link between the good and power is one of the driving ideas of Jacques Lacan's *Seminar VII*, titled *The Ethics of Psychoanalysis*. The good, according to Lacan, is simply the form that power takes. As he points out, "The domain of the good is the

---

6   Michel Foucault, "The Eye of Power," in *Power/Knowledge: Selected Interviews & Other Writings*, trans. Colin Gordon, et al. (New York: Pantheon Books, 1980), 156.

birth of power."[7] The good is not an abstract political ideal but what we have power over and can make use of. In this way, Lacan connects the good as a political ideal with the various goods that we possess. By doing so, he makes it clear that we use the good, just like we use goods, to keep us at a distance from the trauma of enjoyment. Lacan continues in *Seminar VII*, "what is meant by defending one's goods is one and the same thing as forbidding oneself from enjoying them."[8] Eliding the difference between the good and goods enables Lacan to see that the good represents what we cannot enjoy, which is why no political organization, despite Aristotle's influential claim otherwise, has ever pursued it.

The same dynamic holds for power as well. Like the good, power represents an attempt to protect ourselves from enjoyment. Power is power over enjoyment. We look to gain power in order to avoid encountering the enjoyment that threatens to upend our everyday existence. When they attain power, people use it to isolate themselves from others' enjoyment: they buy vast tracts of land, build fences, install alarms, and hire security guards, all so that they can avoid the disturbance that others' enjoyment would introduce through loud music, strange smells, and even intrusion on their property. Power is appealing because enjoyment is threatening. It promises to undermine our psychic equilibrium.

But the problem is that when I put up a gate to keep others out I simultaneously lock myself in. The attempt to use power to safeguard enjoyment ends up suffocating this enjoyment by eliminating the breathing space, the contact with others, that it requires. My own enjoyment is not just my private possession. I cannot hoard it for myself or protect it from the intrusion of others because it depends on my relation to others and to their enjoyment.

---

7 Jacques Lacan, *The Seminar of Jacques Lacan, Book VII: The Ethics of Psychoanalysis, 1959–1960*, trans. Dennis Porter, ed. Jacques-Alain Miller (New York: Norton, 1992), 229.

8 Jacques Lacan, *The Seminar of Jacques Lacan, Book VII*, 230.

It is only by opening myself to the other's enjoyment that I open myself to my own because my enjoyment occurs through the mediation of the other, through how I relate to the enjoying other. This is what Alenka Zupančič gets at in *What IS Sex?* She writes, "Even the most solitary enjoyment presupposes the structure of the Other. This is also why, the more we try to get rid of the Other and become utterly self-dependent, the more we are bound to find something radically heterogeneous ('Other') at the very heart of our most intimate enjoyment. There is no enjoyment without the Other, because all enjoyment originates at the place of the Other (as the locus of signifiers). Our innermost enjoyment can only occur at that 'extimate' place."[9] By keeping the other's enjoyment at bay, one keeps one's own enjoyment at bay as well, which is in fact the point of creating distance from the other.

Like the good, power provides an opportunity for enjoyment only in the negative sense. When one enjoys power, one enjoys giving it up. No one just intelligently holds on to power. As power becomes secure, leaders put it at risk in wars or with actions that can only lead to failure. Leaders constantly work toward their own downfall because work in this direction is the only way to enjoy the power of leadership. When we look at the catastrophic decisions of political leaders in modern world history—Robespierre's turn against Georges Danton and Camille Desmoulins, Lincoln's policy of appeasement with the white South, Lenin's appointment of Stalin as General Secretary, Hitler's invasion of the Soviet Union, or Putin's war in Ukraine, just to name a few—it becomes clear that those in power do not enjoy retaining their power. Of course, there are countless actions that leaders take to hold on to power, but there is nothing enjoyable in this. Even those leaders who retain power for life find ways to put their reign and themselves in jeopardy. The only way to enjoy power is to push it to the point where one either loses it or is on the verge of losing it, which

---

9   Alenka Zupančič, *What IS Sex?* (Cambridge: MIT Press, 2017), 29.

is why Napoleon ended his days not on the throne in Paris but isolated on the island of St. Helena. No conquest is ever enough, not because we strive for infinite power but because enjoyment lies at the moment when the conquest fails. Success is a detour on the path to failure because failure is the site of enjoyment. Power holds enjoyment at a distance but becomes enjoyable at the moments when it is threatened.

Both the good and power serve as lures to obscure the role that enjoyment plays in politics. We take refuge in the idea of the good or the idea of power in order to avoid confronting how we derive enjoyment, which takes something from us rather than giving us anything. We attain the good or accumulate power, but we enjoy through what we lose. We suffer our enjoyment. Just as the good and power provide respite from the disturbance of enjoyment, political theories focused on the good and on power offer the same respite. The structure of enjoyment marks a radical break with the logic of the good articulated by Aristotle and the logic of power articulated by Nietzsche. When we pursue the good or power, we are doing so because they provide fuel for our mode of enjoying, not because they are desirable or enjoyable in themselves. Rather than enjoying the good, we enjoy its sacrifice.[10]

---

10 As Joan Copjec puts it, "The psychoanalytic subject, in short, being subject to a principle *beyond* pleasure, *is not driven to seek his own good.*" Joan Copjec, *Read My Desire*, 87.

7

The Fecklessness
of the Facts

THE POLITICAL PRIORITY OF enjoyment over power and the good renders knowledge ineffective as a political tool. Campaigns for consciousness raising among the oppressed and exploited rarely work. More knowledge almost never proves salutary. This seems odd because those who embrace political positions contrary to their own interests appear so clearly to lack the requisite knowledge that would enable them to act for their own good. If knowledge is lacking, why wouldn't supplying the lacking knowledge be effective? Despite the obviousness of this strategy, recourse to it evinces a misunderstanding of how politics works.

From communist attempts to promote awareness of exploitation among the working class to feminist consciousness-raising groups, knowledge has not been able to dislodge the majoritarian investment in oppressive systems by those who are the victims of them. The problem with raising consciousness is that oppressive situations do not continue due to a lack of knowledge but due to the enjoyment that they produce for both the oppressor and the oppressed. It is this enjoyment that leftist movements must struggle against, not an absence of knowledge.

More knowledge will necessarily backfire unless the prospects for the form of enjoyment changes at the same time. More knowledge can augment the amount of enjoyment that subjects obtain from their disavowal of what they know. Campaigns of information give the subject more opportunity for sacrificing this knowledge in self-destructive acts, and it is sacrifice that produces enjoyment. As anyone who has enjoyed potato chips or a piece of cake knows, the knowledge that these foods are physiologically harmful doesn't detract from the enjoyment of them but augments it. The same logic is at work in politics. We are constantly eating potato chips and cake when making our political decisions, although political theorists tend to believe that we are eating broccoli and brussels sprouts. Rather than trying to do what is good for us, we are trying to find a way to enjoy ourselves.

If I know that a candidate or political position will harm my own interest, this makes supporting them all the more enjoyable, provided that I can disavow the knowledge of this harm and avoid openly confronting it. Just as with junk food, I enjoy how the political position introduces an excess that disturbs the good into my existence. This excess permits me an experience of transcendence in which I go beyond my everyday life.

Enjoyment is an affective response to a situation, not the result of what one knows about one's situation. One of Baruch Spinoza's greatest insights concerns the need to respond to emotions with other, stronger emotions. In his *Ethics*, he states, "*An emotion cannot be checked or destroyed except by a contrary emotion which is stronger than the emotion which is to be checked.*"[1] To those caught up in a conservative form of enjoyment, one must offer some other form of enjoyment that will be more intense. Spinoza specifically warns about the futility to fighting emotions with knowledge, as the Left consistently attempts to do. He proclaims, "*No emotion can be checked by the true knowledge of good and evil in so far as it is true, but only in so far as it is considered as an emotion.*"[2] When we attack an emotional response with knowledge, we do nothing to allay the strength of the emotional response. The only path, as

---

1   Baruch Spinoza, *Ethics*, trans. Samuel Shirley (Indianapolis: Hackett, 1992), 158.

2   Baruch Spinoza, *Ethics*, 161.

Spinoza suggests, is to combat the outburst of enjoyment with a prospect offering more enjoyment.

Sigmund Freud makes a similar point in his brief essay "Wild Psychoanalysis" but ultimately goes even further than Spinoza. He writes this essay after encountering a patient treated by another specialist who tried to cure her by detailing exactly how she repressed her sexuality. This treatment method, which seems like it should work, forces Freud to write up a critique. Freud inveighs against attempts to cure patients by informing them about what they have repressed so that they can escape the neurosis that cripples them. He claims, "Informing the patient of what he does not know because he has repressed it … [has] as much influence on the symptoms of a nervous illness as a distribution of menu-cards in a time of famine has upon hunger."[3] Implicitly following Spinoza, Freud explains here that knowledge does not have the power to counteract the psychic satisfaction that the subject receives from its neurosis. The subject doesn't have a neurosis because it lacks conscious awareness of what it has repressed. The subject lacks conscious awareness of what it has repressed because of the neurosis, because the disorder provides a form of enjoyment that has a hold over the subject.

The attempt to cure a psychic problem with knowledge assumes that it is the absence of knowledge that has created the problem in the first place. One posits that the subject has developed a neurosis as a result of repression. But in fact the causality runs in the opposite direction. Repression emerges in response to the subject's psychic disorder rather than causing the disorder. In attempting to deal directly with it by providing the missing knowledge, one never approaches the level of the problem itself.

---

3   Sigmund Freud, "Wild Psychoanalysis," trans. Joan Riviere, in *The Complete Psychological Works of Sigmund Freud*, ed. James Strachey (London: Hogarth Press, 1957), 11:225.

The same is true with politics. One avoids knowing certain political facts because one adopts a conservative political position. It is not one's lack of knowledge that is to blame for the conservatism. As a result, simply supplying the missing knowledge can no more change someone's political position than it can cure a psychic disorder. Education is not a panacea when what is required is a change in the form of enjoyment that leads to a lack of education.

But wild psychoanalysis or using knowledge as a treatment method is not just an erroneous approach that remains ineffectual. This approach does not just leave things as they are. Freud understands that the attempt to fill in the gaps of the subject's repression with knowledge has the effect of inevitably making things worse. More knowledge alone enhances the disorder. As Freud puts it a bit later in the "Wild Psychoanalysis" essay, "informing the patient of his unconscious regularly results in an intensification of the conflict within him and an exacerbation of his troubles."[4] Confronting the subject with knowledge about what it has repressed prompts the subject to redouble the forces of repression, not to relax them. The disorder requires repression, and until the subject addresses the disorder itself, it will not give up the repression that sustains it. The introduction of knowledge enhances the need for this repression.

Although Freud is talking about the psychic troubles of individual patients, attempts at responding to political problems by supplying knowledge—about who will benefit from tax policies, about how immigrants are not actually stealing jobs, and so on—run into precisely the same problem. This is what becomes self-evident when we examine how the supporters of right-wing populists respond to revelations about such information. Liberals and leftists continually express shock that even more knowledge does not cure the politically sick patient, but the problem is that the patient is not suffering from a knowledge problem. People

4   Sigmund Freud, "Wild Psychoanalysis," 11:225.

become vulnerable to right-wing appeals not because they don't know enough about the situation but because they experience a deficit in enjoyment that the appeals rectify by allowing them to access enjoyment through the figure of the enemy.

It is impossible to stamp out reactionary political appeals by claiming that things should remain as they are and that small technical changes will rectify the situation. A call for a return to moderation will never be successful. This represents a capitulation to the capitalist status quo and simply recreates the dynamic that led to the reactionary political appeal in the first place. When contrasted with the enjoyment-laden rightist project, this invocation of the reality principle will seem a pale alternative.[5]

The first step in combatting right-wing appeals is to provide a different form of enjoyment that trumps both that of capitalism and that of religious or ethnic fundamentalism. This alternate form of enjoyment is that of nonbelonging, that of those who enjoy in solidarity their failure to belong. This mode of enjoyment is more, not less, intense than the xenophobic nationalism of the reactionary Right, but at the same time, it is more difficult to organize because it is not attached to a ready-made identity like ethnicity or nation or religion. Political struggle is the struggle between the direct enjoyment of nonbelonging and the enjoyment of this position through the figure of the enemy. In order to affect this struggle, one must intervene on the terrain of enjoyment rather than that of knowledge. This terrain requires that we confront the existence of social contradictions, where we can see what nonbelonging looks like.

---

5   The moderation of the reality principle was Hillary Clinton's only guiding ideal in the 2016 US Presidential campaign. The failure of this campaign attests to the bankruptcy of the reality principle as a political strategy.

8.

Do I Contradict Myself?

THE ROLE THAT CONTRADICTION plays in the social order and in emancipation becomes clear in the philosophy of Hegel, even if his philosophy itself is not the model of clarity. Although Hegel does not appear as a politically committed thinker relative to Marx, his philosophy actually makes an unsurpassable contribution to the politics of emancipation. Hegel focuses his entire system of thought on uncovering contradictions within existing philosophical systems and within social structures. For Hegel, the point of philosophizing is to work through the contradictions that manifest themselves in order to discover if there is an end to them or not. As a result of this philosophical project, he shows us, in a way that isn't clear to even Hegel himself, the source of emancipatory enjoyment.

Hegel doesn't uncover contradictions with the aim of ultimately eliminating them and creating a philosophy or a society that runs without a hitch. Such an achievement is not only impossible but also unthinkable. Instead of attempting to solve the problem of contradiction, his philosophy engages a series of contradictions to show that no matter how far we take our theoretical or social development, we will never reach the point of overcoming contradiction once and for all. As Hegel tries to show, we cannot overcome contradiction because it is ontologically necessary. Contradiction isn't a barrier that our political acts must try to

eclipse but the foundation for them that they must incorporate and affirm.[1]

The most important political intervention that Hegel makes in his philosophy consists in recognizing contradiction as actual. For Hegel, both the social order and subjectivity are inevitably contradictory entities. Even though they may appear to strive to overcome contradiction, it remains fundamental because it is the condition of possibility for all activity. In contrast to how the majority of interpreters have received his thought, Hegel does not imagine that every contradiction between a thesis and its antithesis must be resolved into a synthesis.[2] Instead, he insists that contradictions actually exist and sustain themselves, leading not to their synthesis in a higher truth but to increasingly recalcitrant contradictions. The dialectical movement that he theorizes depends not on overcoming contradictions but on their persistence.

Things are contradictory insofar as they are never simply themselves but are always implicated in what is other to them. This is clear in the case of animals that ingest otherness through breathing and eating and yet remain themselves. Even inanimate

---

1   Hegel's attitude toward contradiction provides a different way of conceptualizing emancipation from that of Marx. For Marx, we move in the direction of emancipation when we overcome contradictions and, in the end, when we arrive at a social order no longer beset by them at all. Although his vision of the communist future is not utopian, it is a vision in which contradictions dissipate so that differences can flower. The implicit political project of Hegel envisions historical advances through deepening contradictions rather than eliminating them. His philosophy culminates in the absolute, which is the reconciliation (*Versöhnung*) with contradiction rather than its definitive overcoming.

2   One of the terrible ironies in the reception of Hegel is that the thinker the most committed to contradiction has become identified with its overcoming through a process leading from thesis to antithesis to synthesis. Such a process has absolutely nothing to do with Hegel's thought, and he never even uses these terms that are so often associated with him.

objects aren't entirely distinct from their surroundings but take on a certain shape on the basis of their environment. Things are what they are, for Hegel, but they are also what they are not, which is why he sees everything as fundamentally contradictory. The law of identity, A=A, is a fantasy that extrapolates from the structure of how things actually are and how they are inherently involved in what is other. As Hegel himself infelicitously puts it, identity is not just identity alone but the identity of identity and difference. This process reaches its culminating point in subjectivity, which has the ability not just to suffer its contradictions but to think them. The act of thinking, for Hegel, is an act of apprehending contradiction in thought, which Hegel names spirit or *Geist*.

Hegel conceives of his project as one of speculative thinking, which is thinking that pays attention to and nourishes itself on contradiction. He contrasts this with ordinary thinking, which founders on contradiction. When it encounters a contradiction, ordinary thinking assumes that it has made an error. In *The Science of Logic*, Hegel describes this distinction. He states, "*Speculative thought* consists only in this, in holding firm to contradiction and to itself in the contradiction, but not in the sense that, as it happens in ordinary thought, it would let itself be ruled by it and allow it to dissolve its determinations into just other determinations or into nothing."[3] Here, there is no thought of overcoming contradiction through progress. The point is rather "holding firm" to it, which is what Hegel attempts throughout his philosophy.

Holding firm to contradiction is not just Hegel's philosophical project. It is also a political project of emancipation. Every social order has contradictions that threaten to break the society apart. By engaging in a dialectical analysis of the contradictions, we can see how the dissolution of one contradiction causes the emergence of another that is more recalcitrant. This is the process

---

3   G. W. F. Hegel, *The Science of Logic*, trans. George Di Giovanni (Cambridge: Cambridge University Press, 2010), 383.

that Hegel chronicles in *The Phenomenology of Spirit* and *The Science of Logic*. For instance, the *Phenomenology* begins with the contradiction that besets sense certainty. Sense certainty is a position that rejects universals for the sake of the certainty of immediate sense experience, and yet in order to describe immediate sense experience, this position requires the use of universals. The unfolding of this contradiction leads to the next dialectical moment—perception, which openly employs universals and thus reveals itself as more difficult to undermine than sense certainty. This process goes on to the point of absolute knowing, which is the point where contradiction appears as unsurpassable and thus integrated into thinking itself.

In each of Hegel's philosophical works, the absolute is reconciliation with contradiction. This is a political end point at which one attains universality and recognizes that universality involves contradiction. As Hegel conceives it, the universal does not represent the overcoming of all contradiction but the recognition of its necessity. This represents a radical position because it deflates the status of authority that inegalitarian society requires. Inequality depends on a belief in the possibility of overcoming contradiction. In contrast, no one can have a hierarchical position above others if no one escapes contradiction. Freedom and equality emerge as actual through this recognition.

For Hegel, contradiction is just a fundamental principle of thinking and of existence. What he doesn't see—because he doesn't have access to the insights of psychoanalysis—is that contradiction is also the way that the subject enjoys. We are drawn to contradiction not just because it is evident when we attempt to establish a complete systematic account of the whole but because enjoyment occurs at the site of contradiction. The contradictory point of any structure is the point at which it ceases to contain all possibilities and opens up to what the structure itself implies but cannot include. This is what occurs, for instance, when the contradictions of capitalist society point to an egalitarianism that it cannot attain. Such an opening indicates the inherent radicality to contradiction: it places one in a position of excess relative to the structure that produces it. The experience of this excess is enjoyment.

Enjoyment occurs at the position of contradiction where the social order reaches its internal point of failure. Enjoyment is inextricable from the existence of contradictions where it can take place. Were there no actual contradictions, there would be no opening for enjoyment. Existence within the social order would be fully determined and utterly tedious.

The relationship between contradiction and enjoyment is clearest in the explosions of enjoyment that occur when impossible political events transpire. In terms of the political field at the time of its outbreak, the French Revolution was an impossible event. Social relations had been fixed for centuries. The ruling structure had not only been solidifying over time but had a divine endorsement. To challenge the authority of the king, the aristocracy, and the clergy was to call into question not just a political organization but the ontological foundation of the world, grounded in theology.

The rigidity of the European social structure made revolutionary change impossible. But the French Revolution nevertheless took place. It could only occur thanks to the contradictions of the French social order at the time, which created the political space for the impossible to happen. It required not just famine, but famine that occurred during a time of burgeoning population and new prosperity. This contradiction—famine amid prosperity—made an impossibility, the overthrow of the regime, become thinkable as a possibility. The impossible became possible when the Revolution occurred. It also became visible as the site where one could access the enjoyment that is impossible within the ruling political field of the time. The situation ruled out what the political event actually accomplishes.[4]

The impossibility of the event is evident in Louis XVI's inability to consider that a revolution might take place. It didn't appear to him as present within the field of possibilities, as a famous exchange between the king and Duke La Rochefoucauld revealed. After the storming of the Bastille, Louis XVI famously asked the duke if the people were revolting. La Rochefoucauld responded, "Non, sire, c'est une révolution." By classifying the event as a revolt, the king attempted to contain it within the realm of the possible, as an incident that could fit without contradiction in the ruling political framework. This was the only means he had for apprehending what was going on. But by negating Louis XVI's claim and declaring the event a revolution, Duke La Rochefoucauld attested to its position outside this framework. The duke placed the storming of the Bastille in the space of contradiction, a space in which the revolutionaries were enjoying their act of exceeding the existing order. The storming of the Bastille occurred at the point where the French social order's contradictions created an opening for the impossible to happen. It was not possible within prerevolutionary French society to act against the prison that stood for the absolute power of the regime to do as it wanted with its political opponents. But the people

---

4   I owe these terms—*event* and *situation*—to Alain Badiou, who describes the relationship between the event and situation in *Being and Event*, where he lays out his philosophical project. But Badiou doesn't see the situation as inherently contradictory in the way that Hegel does. For him, the situation opens up the possibility for the event through the void that inhabits it. He states, "the void, which is the name of inconsistency in the situation (under the law of the count-as-one), cannot, in itself, be presented or fixed." Alain Badiou, *Being and Event*, trans. Oliver Feltham (New York: Continuum, 2005), 93. The void marks the inconsistency of the situation and thus holds open the space for the event to intervene.

stormed the Bastille anyway because the authority it represented became vulnerable.

The Bastille itself was a contradictory site within the monarchical French social order. It was at once the symbol of the monarchy's absolute power to imprison people in horrible conditions and a site of vulnerability, which is why the people were able to take possession of it. The absolute control that the prison had over its prisoners led the authorities to mistake this control for strength against potential attackers. In this way, the power of the authorities over the prisoners was the mark of the Bastille's weakness.

This contradiction made the Bastille into a site of enjoyment for those who attacked it. By taking up arms against this symbol of absolute power, the revolutionaries enjoyed doing the impossible, gaining a victory against a seemingly indomitable force. The revolutionaries who seized the prison did so replete with the enjoyment that emanated from the impossibility of their act. As they embarked on their historic attack, they touched the point at which the determinations of their social order could no longer contain them. No matter what their private feelings were at the moment of the attack, they placed themselves structurally at the site of enjoyment. Their revolution was driven by an enjoyment of transcendence through the encounter with a social contradiction.

This emancipatory enjoyment is not confined to acts of direct political action like the storming of the Bastille. Galileo experienced a scientific version of the same enjoyment when he defied the Catholic authorities and offered definitive proof that movement in the supposedly eternal heavenly spheres confirmed the heliocentric theory of the solar system.[5] In the manner of

---

5   Even though Copernicus initially launched the geocentric theory, Galileo's version of it caused much more consternation among Church authorities. Copernicus caused almost no disruption at all because these authorities treated his system as simply a different form of calculation for planetary

the French revolutionaries, Galileo acted through the opening provided by the contradictions that he encountered. The Aristotelian and Ptolemaic geocentric systems had points of contradiction where their explanations for the universe broke down. These contradictions offered Galileo sites of intervention where he could propose an alternative. Without these contradictions, there would be no space for an appealing alternative explanation to emerge. The appeal depends on the contradictions in the ruling system because the contradictions are the point where one enjoys. One could simply pose an alternative, but there would be no way to register the alternative as a possible site for enjoyment, which is what Galileo is able to do.

This is why the heliocentric paradigm that Aristarchus of Samos proposed in the third century BCE attracted no major adherents. When Aristarchus argued for his alternative to the Aristotelean geocentric system, he was not, in contrast to Galileo, responding to contradictions evident within that system. Even though today we would say that Aristarchus was correct and Aristotle was wrong, Aristarchus failed to provide a way to mobilize enjoyment through contradiction, which is why his heliocentric theory could not make any inroads against the Aristotelean geocentric one. At the time, the Aristotelean system actually explained the movements of heavenly bodies better than the geocentric model that Aristarchus put forward. Aristarchus simply proposed an alternative to the prevailing theory but created no engagement with the contradictions of the ruling system. Galileo provides a revelatory contrast. He not only developed his

---

motion. As Steven Weinberg points out, "it was still possible for the church to tolerate the Copernican system as a purely mathematical device for calculating apparent motions of planets, though not as a theory of the real nature of the planets and their motions." Steven Weinberg, *To Explain the World: The Discovery of Modern Science* (New York: HarperCollins, 2015), 182. Once Galileo shows the empirical evidence for the theory with the orbits of Jupiter's moons, this tolerance ceases to remain possible.

heliocentrism in response to contradictions becoming apparent in the geocentric conceptions, but he also reacted to the existence of two contradictory geocentric theories, the Ptolemaic theory and the Aristotelean.[6] Although these often become grouped together as geocentrism when people discuss the history of astronomy, they were distinct theories that could not be reconciled with each other. Each theory had internal contradictions, and each relied on a structure that contradicted the other theory. These were contradictions that did not yet exist for Aristarchus, since the Aristotelean conception had just come into existence and Ptolemy had yet to be born. Aristarchus, in contrast to Galileo, gave would-be followers nothing to enjoy in his theory, which is why he was stuck with would-be followers instead of actual followers and why his conception of heliocentrism went nowhere.[7]

The point of the contradiction in a system is the point at which one can enjoy transcending the limits that the system imposes on what is possible. When one takes up this position, one identifies with the position of nonbelonging, even if one is a renowned scientist. To explore the point of contradiction in a system is not the same as having an orgasm, but it nonetheless provides access to enjoyment. This is why scientists like Galileo find exploring the contradictions of the prevailing system worthy of pursuit. It is not the drive for knowledge but the experience of enjoyment that guides such research. Or, the experience of

---

6   The fact that there were two competing geocentric paradigms is often forgotten, but this is crucial for Galileo's intervention. If there were only one, the contradictions would have been much less evident.

7   In *The Structure of Scientific Revolutions*, Thomas Kuhn argues similarly, although without any reference to enjoyment. According to Kuhn, a new theory can take hold only after the point at which a sufficient number of anomalies develop within the dominant theory. The anomalies create an opening for the new paradigm to emerge, and this opening did not exist for Aristarchus because astronomers had yet to find inexplicable anomalies in the Aristotelean system.

enjoyment undergirds the drive for knowledge, making it seem worthwhile to the scientist. The ability to occupy the point of contradiction is what makes all revolutionary change appealing and enjoyable. Galileo found an enjoyment in going beyond geocentrism. His discovery not only provided empirical evidence in support of geocentrism. It also exposed a contradiction by showing movement in the unmoving eternal spheres.

Galileo's enjoyment of the contradiction is precisely what drove the Inquisition to crack down on him. The Inquisition sensed the threat that Galileo's enjoyment of the contradiction posed to the Church's monopoly on enjoyment. He died under house arrest in 1642 as a result of the menace that his alternative form of enjoyment posed to that of the Church. The fact that Galileo's proof put his life in danger—or at least seemed to, because it's not entirely clear that the threat was genuinely mortal—attests to the enjoyment inherent in his position. Asserting the proof for heliocentrism amid the ruling geocentric structure brought with it a scientific version of the enjoyment evident in the storming of the Bastille.

Enjoyment represents the great political force because it drives people to act in ways that go beyond what the ruling political order would allow. Enjoyment emerges from the contradictions of the ruling system and occurs through attaining a point of excess relative to that system. While this positioning gives enjoyment an inherent radicality, it can always be marshalled for conservative or reactionary purposes if it becomes identified with an enemy. But this requires deviating from its basic disruptiveness. When we enjoy, we touch the sky, reaching it via the contradictions that beset the social order and going beyond what the society envisions as possible. With the development of heliocentrism, Galileo didn't just change the course of the world. He offered a way of enjoying that posed a radical threat to the Catholic Church's rule, which relied, like every form of rule, on obscuring its contradictions and diverting its followers from the enjoyment of these contradictions. The Church demanded that transcendence be limited to the divine with the Church itself in charge of policing access to this realm. But Galileo revealed that transcendence was immanent to the social order, located at the point of contradiction. Although we think of Galileo as a scientist fighting against religious dogmatism, he is also a figure of enjoyment who created a theory that appealed because it occupied a contradictory point within the ruling social and scientific structure.

This enjoyment of the impossible is also evident in acts that we observe, not just what we do. One need not be Galileo defying geocentrism and the Church in order to access it. When we witness an act that transcends our expectations of what is possible in a given situation, this is also a source of enjoyment and can teach us a political lesson. Such acts take place at the point of contradiction, where what cannot happen does happen. One of the great appeals of sports spectatorship is the ability to enjoy watching impossibilities occur. On the one hand, sports provide parochial pleasures for fans. One identifies with an individual or team and takes pleasure in the victories that they achieve over the enemy. There is nothing at all radical about this dimension of sports fandom. Because it relies on the distinction between the friend and enemy, it actually contributes to conservative politics. As a fan, one experiences a sense of belonging relative to the outsiders who root for other teams. This belonging also fuels the capitalist system, as team owners and individual players make millions on the basis of fan devotion. All this places sports on the side of political conservatism. On the other hand, however, there are moments in sports that go beyond mere pleasure and produce a transcendent enjoyment. These are secular miracles, times when an athlete or group of athletes accomplish what seems not to be possible. Unlike the pleasure that accompanies watching one's favorite player or team win a game, the occurrence of an impossibility—a dramatic upset, a dominating victory, an unsurpassable record, or the defiance of injury—brings enjoyment to spectators.[8] What makes these events enjoyable is that they involve suffering both for the athlete and for the spectator as they confront the imminence of failure.

We can see the miraculous in events such as Muhammad Ali using an unforeseen rope-a-dope strategy to defeat the heavily favored George Foreman in Zaire, Martina Navratilova's six consecutive Wimbledon titles in tennis, Bob Beamon's setting the long jump record by more than two feet beyond the existing one at the 1968 Olympics, and Willis Reed's ability to lead the New York Knicks to victory in a 1970 NBA Finals game despite suffering from a torn thigh muscle.[9] In each case, the spectators who saw these events could find enjoyment in them because they were watching the impossible happen. The athletes managed to do what seemed like it couldn't be done. These were moments of contradiction: they were structurally impossible, and yet they occurred nonetheless. The achievements went beyond what defined the possible at the time, which is why they brought so much enjoyment to spectators. When these events occurred, the conservative pleasure of sporting spectatorship—rooting for one's own side to win—gave way to the enjoyment of the impossible. One watches sporting events in large part for such moments when a miraculous performance occurs. Even though sporting events occur within the framework of the social order and bring great wealth to already wealthy capitalists, some performances depart

---

8   For an excellent analysis of the political and existential radicality of sports fandom—how this fandom produces enjoyment through loss rather than through success—see Joseph Reynoso, "Boston Sucks! A Psychoanalysis of Sports," *Psychoanalysis, Culture & Society* (2021): 1–17.

9   It is tempting to add to this list the racehorse Secretariat's 1973 victory by a record-setting 31 lengths in record-setting time, a margin of victory and a time that no horse has come close to matching till this day. But I will confine myself to human examples and not mention it.

from the social framework completely and allow spectators to enjoy a contradictory transcendence.[10]

Although provincial or even nationalist forces often try to direct the enjoyment of the sporting event to conservative ends, the impossibility of the event reveals its link to emancipation. Every sporting event is not a competition between two individuals or teams. It is a competition between the rightist form of enjoyment that dwells in the opposition between the competitors and the emancipatory form that occurs when the impossible happens. As we witness the sporting miracle, we occupy the point of social contradiction just as we would when engaging in radical political activity. Obviously, there is a difference between watching the World Cup and storming the Bastille, but not as much as one might think. The chill that we experience when watching the great sporting achievement is the result of a radical enjoyment, the enjoyment of seeing the impossible actually happen, which is what aligns it with storming the Bastille. Sport has the ability to take spectators beyond all expectations of what is possible, which is the driving reason why people watch sporting events. Even any ordinary game often includes one or two extraordinary moments where an athlete defies the possibilities and enables spectators to partake in the impossible.[11]

---

10 The fact that a transcendent event can occur in the realm of sports indicates that we should expand Alain Badiou's number of truth procedures that serve as the site for events. According to Badiou, there are political events, scientific events, artistic events, and love events. That's it. Despite finding the paradigm for the event in Paul's ministry, Badiou rules out the possibility of a religious event because, he claims, there is no truth in religion. He is silent about sports. He rules out economic events because, in his view, economic activity is purely animalistic.

11 As I was writing this, Justin Tucker, the kicker for the Baltimore Ravens, an American football team, kicked a record-setting 66-yard field goal. Even though this kick brought victory to the rival of the team I support, I nonetheless began wildly cheering the event with my son. The enjoyment of experiencing the impossible trumped the pleasure of our rooting interest.

The example of sports indicates that the impossible is not reserved for the privileged few. The enjoyment of the impossible point of contradiction is not just confined to political actors such as Robespierre or scientists like Galileo or writers such as Toni Morrison. This enjoyment is always universal, even if one specific person accomplishes the act that makes it available. We are drawn to the impossible point of contradiction because it is the unique site for access to enjoyment.

Perhaps the best example of how contradiction brings enjoyment is that of love. While one can easily imagine explanations of love that reduce it to self-interest or to narcissistic gratification, love also involves the total disruption of one's identity for the sake of someone else.[12] When one loves, one values the beloved more than oneself, so that one's sense of who one is lies in the other's power. The beloved has the ability to wreak absolute devastation on the lover, while also being the source of an unsurpassed enjoyment. This is the basic contradiction of love: the other brings me great enjoyment only insofar as this other can destroy the basis of my subjectivity. To love is to grant the other an absolute power over one's own subjectivity. If one doesn't grant the other this power, if one holds back a bit, then one cheats oneself out of love's satisfactions. One can only enjoy love if one submits to love's contradiction.

Even though love gives the other power to destroy one's subjectivity, it is the subject itself that is the source of this valuing of the other. The beloved counts for more than the subject thanks to the

---

It was a moment when emancipation won out over conservative sports spectatorship.

12 For instance, Søren Kierkegaard claims that "erotic love is one of the very strongest and deepest expressions of selfishness." Søren Kierkegaard, *For Self-Examination*, in *For Self-Examination and Judge For Yourself!*, trans. Howard V. Hong and Edna H. Hong (Princeton: Princeton University Press, 1990), 78. Even though Kierkegaard advocates the possibility of a genuine love for God, erotic love, as he sees it (sadly for Regine Olsen), necessarily expresses just the desire to be loved.

subject's own act of sublimation, which gives the beloved this value. Love devalues the self in relation to the other by giving the self the power to enact this devaluation, which is why the experience of love involves the subject in contradiction. I must have the ability to give the other more value than I give to myself. The foundational contradiction in love is the source of its enjoyment. Love provides enjoyment rather than pleasure. While surely there are pleasurable moments in a love relation, love is primarily an affair of enjoyment.

The contrast between the pleasures of everyday life—or the absence of them—and the enjoyment of love comes through in the great English love poetry of the seventeenth century. From Shakespeare to John Donne, the love poets of this epoch highlight this contrast. In Sonnet 29, for instance, Shakespeare lays out his everyday unpleasure before turning to the enjoyment of his beloved that causes this unpleasure to sink into the background. He writes,

> When, in disgrace with fortune and men's eyes,
> I all alone beweep my outcast state
> And trouble deaf heaven with my bootless cries
> And look upon myself and curse my fate,
> Wishing me like to one more rich in hope,
> Featured like him, like him with friends possess'd,
> Desiring this man's art and that man's scope,
> With what I most enjoy contented least;
> Yet in these thoughts myself almost despising,
> Haply I think on thee, and then my state,
> Like to the lark at break of day arising
> From sullen earth, sings hymns at heaven's gate;
> For thy sweet love remember'd such wealth brings
> That then I scorn to change my state with kings.[13]

---

13   William Shakespeare, Sonnet 29.

Love completely changes the valence of everything else in the po-et's life. He begins "almost despising" himself, which reveals the suffering that love brings. But it also leads him to a point where he wouldn't change positions with a king. Love debases everything else of value in the lover's existence. It also elevates the subject to an unparalleled experience. This contradiction of love is the source of the unparalleled enjoyment that it provides. While the lover ex-periences untold misery, no one in love would ever change places with someone in a more pleasant situation that lacked this love.

Our attraction to love is simultaneously our attraction to the enjoyment of contradiction. Being in love is enjoyable because it is contradictory. To subtract the self-debasing quality from love would be to destroy the love experience altogether. One must suf-fer in love, or one is not really in love. This is due to the extreme valuation of the love object. In love, the other holds the fate of the lover in its hands. The lover invests this object with so much passion that everything else begins to pale in comparison. Love debases because it elevates.

We should not be surprised that Hegel developed his grasp of conceptual thinking out of his understanding of love. For He-gel, love goes out of itself to embrace the other. In *The Philosophy of Right*, Hegel claims, "Love is … the most immense contradiction; the understanding cannot solve it, because there is nothing more intractable than this punctiliousness of the self-consciousness which is negated and which I ought nevertheless to possess as an affirmative."[14] We can say exactly the same thing about Hegel's ver-sion of the concept. For Hegel, conceptual thinking must include itself and the other's difference together. The concept doesn't re-duce what is other to the structure of thought but brings the two

---

14 G. W. F. Hegel, *Elements of the Philosophy of Right*, trans. H. B. Nisbet, ed. Al-len W. Wood (Cambridge: Cambridge University Press, 1991), 199 (trans-lation slightly modified).

together in a contradictory unity. Both love and the concept are the contradictory identity of identity and difference.

As Hegel shows, contradiction is not what we must overcome to create an emancipated society but the basis for such a society. Hierarchical social structures depend on the repression of contradiction in order to sustain themselves: for instance, imperial societies claim to eliminate social contradictions through obedience to the leader, while capitalism presents itself as capable of overcoming contradiction through infinite accumulation. In both cases, the point is hiding contradiction rather than confronting it. It is not contradiction but the failure to reconcile ourselves with contradiction that bars the path to an emancipated society. It is due to the contradictions of the social order that we are not just the determinate products of this order but free. Emancipation is not emancipation from contradiction but into it. The radical political act occurs through the enjoyment of contradiction.

Rather than imagining a future in which we emancipate ourselves out of contradiction, we should reverse these terms. Emancipation occurs when we are reconciled with the necessity of contradiction, not when we transcend it. As long as we hold out the hope for creating a noncontradictory society, we will remain susceptible to the problem of emancipatory projects turning into their opposite. When it proves impossible to overcome contradiction—as it necessarily must, since contradiction is structurally necessary for every society and every form of subjectivity—leftist leaders will try to identify an enemy responsible for contradiction's persistence. Once the search for an enemy begins, they leave the project of emancipation behind and implicitly embark on the conservative one of turning contradiction into opposition. It is only by holding firm to contradiction that we sustain a genuinely leftist enjoyment.

9.

Breaking
the Law

ENJOYMENT TRANSCENDS THE CONFINES of the social order, but it doesn't transgress the law that constitutes this order. Since enjoyment occurs through excess, it seems to make sense that one could find enjoyment only in exceeding the restrictions of the law, in going beyond what the social order prohibits. Transgression appears as the path to emancipation, which is why so many leftists invest themselves in adopting various forms of transgression for the sake of transgression. To violate the restrictions that the law imposes is certainly to achieve a certain form of excess—an excess relative to the law. But this excess is not the site of radical enjoyment. In the act of going beyond the limit of the law, one often remains within socially determined possibilities. The limits of the law are not the limits of the social situation.[1]

---

1   One line of thought that focuses on the oppressiveness of the law is the critique of biopower, advanced by Michel Foucault, Giorgio Agamben, and Roberto Esposito, among many others. Agamben, for instance, envisions an emancipatory future where we will not be completely rid of law but will no longer have to deal with its constraint. He writes, "One day humanity will play with law just as children play with dis-used objects, not in order to restore them to their canonical use but to free them from it for good." Giorgio Agamben, *State of Exception*, trans. Kevin Attell (Chicago: University of Chicago Press, 2005), 64. Agamben has a sense of the law as a barrier to emancipation, which is a popular position on the contemporary Left, even if no one else would articulate this position in the way that Agamben does here.

One of the most grievous errors that undermines the emancipatory project is mistaking transgression for transcendence when interpreting enjoyment. There is nothing inherently radical or emancipatory about transgression. Although people tend to think of famous transgressors in history as paragons of radicality, transgression most often has a conservative function. Rather than exposing the contradiction in the ruling order, transgression typically establishes a clear opposition between the social order and the criminal violating its edicts. Through transgression, emancipatory contradiction becomes conservative opposition between the friends of the social order and its enemies who transgress its edicts. To laud transgression instead of insisting on transcendence as the emancipatory form of enjoyment is to fall for the lure of the criminal.

The criminal's seduction of the Left begins in earnest with Romanticism. Although it takes different forms, the primary strain of Romanticism transforms the criminal or villain into the hero of its political philosophy. The criminal asserts the right of the individual against the dictates of the social order and refuses to compromise a particular form of subjectivity with these dictates. The defiance of the criminal represents the assertion of the individual's value in the face of social conformity. This defiance animates the Romantic project. This is apparent in the celebration of the radicality of Satan in John Milton's *Paradise Lost*. Anyone who reads *Paradise Lost* will find Satan's defiance compelling. He is the one character in the epic poem who exhibits courage, who acts regardless of the personal consequences, in contrast with the calculated behavior of God and Christ.[2] But the seductiveness of

---

2 Milton gives Satan all the best lines and reserves none for God or Christ. In the first book alone, Satan proclaims, "The mind is its own place, and in itself / Can make a heav'n of hell, a hell of heav'n." John Milton, *Paradise Lost*, 2nd ed., ed. Scott Elledge (New York: Norton, 1993), 1:254–255. Satan's character stands out through his refusal to kowtow to God's whims, which seem, as Milton illustrates them, arbitrary and capricious.

Satan doesn't just lead Adam and Eve astray. It also lures Romantic poets to the celebration of transgression as a radical act.

For someone like William Blake, Satan's refusal to heed God's law renders him more attractive than Christ. He sees Milton's poem as an inadvertent tribute to Satan, a tribute that violated Milton's own conscious intentions. In his poem "The Marriage of Heaven and Hell," Blake famously writes, "The reason Milton wrote in fetters when he wrote of Angels and God, and at liberty when of Devils and Hell, is because he was a true poet, and of the Devil's party without knowing it."[3] Blake sees Satan as Milton's unconscious hero because Milton depicts him in such courageous terms. As Milton intimates in the poem, Satan engages in a revolt against the divine, the most powerful being in the universe, which is necessarily doomed to failure. Even though Milton describes the battle taking place, the conclusion is evident from the outset, given God's status as the almighty. By rebelling against the omnipotent, Satan gains our sympathy. Not only is he courageous and defiant, but he is also the prohibitive underdog, in the position of a little league team challenging the 1927 New York Yankees. Blake falls for Satan because he sees not just rebellion but a politically inspired struggle against the oppressiveness of unquestioned authority.

But *Paradise Lost*, despite its great merits as a poem, is not a political guidebook. Blake rightly sees that Satan is Milton's secret hero, but he doesn't see the restricted status of this heroism. What limits—or even eliminates—the radicality of Satan's revolt is that the enjoyment driving this revolt depends on his opposition to God. The dependence on God leaves Satan unable to found his own alternative regime. Even though he rules in Hell, the order there is organized around opposition to the divine. Were there no God to defy, Satan's courageous stand could not exist. His defiance needs the figure of authority that it opposes.

---

3   William Blake, "The Marriage of Heaven and Hell."

Because it relies on the structure of opposition, Satan's regime is a fundamentally conservative one. Whereas reactionary political parties in Europe rely on the opposition to the immigrant to structure their enjoyment, Satan relies on his defiance of God. If Satan did not have God as the enemy, his position would be entirely bereft of enjoyment. The reliance on the enemy reveals the bankruptcy of Satan's political program just as it does that of Alternative für Deutschland.[4]

Satan's position, just like the leftist proponent of the radicality of transgression, is a perverse one. It seeks enjoyment through provoking the master and wants to partake of the master's enjoyment. This is why Satan perversely proclaims, "Evil be thou my good."[5] By transforming evil into a form of good that he pursues, Satan condemns himself and his followers to a parasitical form of enjoyment, the form of enjoyment endemic to the Right. As much as any right-wing political figure, Satan enjoys through his enemy.

Rather than asserting an autonomous enjoyment, an enjoyment of freedom that emancipates, this position contents itself with dependence on the other. This dependence is evident when Satan states,

> To do aught good never will be our task,
> But ever to do ill our sole delight,
> As being the contrary to his high will
> Whom we resist. If then his providence
> Out of our evil seek to bring forth good,

---

4   Although Satan famously proclaims, "Better to reign in hell, than serve in heav'n," he nonetheless has no proposal for how to reign other than to oppose God. John Milton, *Paradise Lost*, 2nd ed., ed. Scott Elledge (New York: Norton, 1993), 1:263. It is an utterly reactive alternative—and thus not an alternative at all.

5   Milton, *Paradise Lost*, 4:10.

Our labor must be to pervert that end,
And out of good still to find means of evil.[6]

Satan's mention of perverting God's ends here is not coincidental. His total commitment to transgression is at once a commitment to a perverse form of enjoyment, an enjoyment that gets off on the other enjoying. Unfortunately, the turn to perversion is not confined to Satan rebelling in Milton's epic. It has infiltrated leftist politics since the Romantic period.

Romanticism's idealization of Satan resounds up to the present. The figure of Satan reappears in that of the criminal figure who defies the law and wins the hearts of the public. It exists in Honoré de Balzac's celebration of the superhuman criminal Vautrin in *Père Goriot*, Fydor Dostoevsky's depiction of Stavrogin in *The Demons*, Friedrich Nietzsche's encomium to the Übermensch, the public adoration of criminals like John Dillinger in the 1930s, the celebration of Bonnie and Clyde in Arthur Penn's 1967 film, and the popularity of Hannibal Lecter in the novels of Thomas Harris. It continues in recent times with the celebration of the figure of the Joker (Joachim Phoenix) in Todd Phillips' risible *The Joker* (2019). The appeal of all these criminal figures repeats that of Milton's Satan. They seem to challenge the dangers of conformity to capitalist society by turning to a life of crime. Some of them go further than others in the extremity of their crimes, with Stravrogin raping a young girl and driving her to suicide and Lecter eating his victims. But in each case, these criminals pursue the perverse enjoyment of transgression in lieu of a radical act.

As a figure of enjoyment, the criminal pales in comparison with the radical political actor. The criminal's transgressions remain within the confines of the social order's possibilities, even though the criminal does violate the law. The radical political act, in contrast, registers as an impossibility within the social order. It

---

6   Milton, *Paradise Lost*, 1:159–165.

is radical because it is impossible, and because it is impossible, it unleashes enjoyment. The authentic political act delivers enjoyment through its ability to inhabit the society's point of contradiction. Its transcendence of the field of social possibilities is the measure of the enjoyment contained within it.

The radicality of transgression is even dwarfed by the simple act of falling in love. The lovers who enjoy the contradiction of love access an enjoyment beyond their social situation in a way that the most transgressive criminal does not. The criminal stays within the social situation because the criminal finds enjoyment through perverting the dictates of the social authority. The lover exists at the point where these dictates become contradictory, akin to the position of the radical political actor.

Transgression is always possible. Even though it can disturb hierarchies and even disrupt the functioning of the social order if it becomes too widespread, transgression lacks genuine radicality. There is a difference between shoplifting and joining an emancipatory political movement. The shoplifter breaks the law but obeys the imperative of capitalist society, while the political actor adheres to the law but defies capitalism's imperative to accumulate. By associating transgression with enjoyment, we fail to see the difference between social authority and the law. Social authority often commands disobedience to the law for the sake of proving one's belonging to the society. This is most clearly evident when we transgress the speed limit. Doing so heeds the dictates of the social authority while violating those of the law. For this reason, transgression can provide a sense of belonging, but it cannot touch the enjoyment of contradiction that emancipation enables.

The response to the Covid-19 pandemic makes clear that transgression of the law harbors no inherent emancipatory potential. Transgressions of laws calling for masks became commonplace. Often those resisting the supposed tyranny of mask laws resorted to violence in order to express their refusal to capitulate in the name of their personal freedom. A purely perverse enjoyment fueled this refusal of the law. The transgressors defied the law in the name of resisting authority, but this same authority is a necessary enemy for the transgressors' position.

Transgression is politically up in the air. There are times when emancipation must transgress an oppressive law. Even then, transgression itself can never become the site of enjoyment for the leftist project. Transgression cannot become an end itself. For the Left, it is only a means to be used and then discarded when no longer necessary.[7] Its need for an enemy makes it clear that transgression cannot become an emancipatory form of enjoyment.

The form that enjoyment takes provides a way to think about what emancipation looks like. It is inherently universal and egalitarian because it emanates from the site of contradiction, the point where no social authority rules. There can be no egalitarian master, no authority who bestows recognition on those who belong. There is only an enjoyment of nonbelonging that derives from social contradiction and the impossibilities that contradiction generates. One can orient the social order by taking the point of contradiction as the locus for the order. This is the challenge for a society of emancipation.

---

7   Georg Lukács counsels a radical indifference toward the legality or illegality of leftist acts. In *History and Class Consciousness*, he writes, "The risk of breaking the law should not be regarded any differently than the risk of missing a train connection when on an important journey." Georg Lukács, *History and Class Consciousness: Studies in Marxist Dialectics*, trans. Rodney Livingstone (Cambridge: MIT Press, 1971), 263.

10

The End of the World
as We Know It

SCIENCE FICTION OFTEN EXPOSES the contradictions of the contemporary social order by extrapolating them into the future. In a way that realist works cannot, science fiction can often show what seems to be impossible to show. To this end, it is not surprising that the first interracial kiss on network television occurred on the science fiction series *Star Trek* and not in a realist drama. The confrontation with the impossible is the preoccupation of science fiction as a genre, which is what gives the genre its potential for radicality.[1] We can look to science fiction as a guide for what leftist political enjoyment might look like, but we must look carefully.

One can measure our contemporary political befuddlement by the relative esteem that greeted two science fiction films that came out in 1999, which was undoubtedly the greatest year for cinema in all of its history.[2] Philosophers and political thinkers of all

---

1   In his work on science fiction, Fredric Jameson stresses the political revelation inherent in this genre, a revelation tied to bringing out hidden contradictions. Jameson writes, we must "assert that not only the production of the unresolvable contradiction is the fundamental process, but that we must imagine some form of gratification inherent in this very confrontation with pessimism and the impossible." Fredric Jameson, *Archaeologies of the Future: The Desire Called Utopia and Other Science Fictions* (London: Verso, 2005), 84. What Jameson puts his finger on here—the encounter with contradiction—is the key to the enjoyment that science fiction provides.

2   A partial list of the masterpieces produced in 1999 includes David Fincher's *Fight Club*, Michael Mann's *The Insider*, Spike Lee's *Summer of Sam*, Stanley Kubrick's *Eyes Wide Shut*, Sofia Coppola's *The Virgin Suicides*, Roger

stripes celebrated *The Matrix* (Lana and Lilly Wachowski, 1999) for its depiction of emancipation through the figure of Neo (Keanu Reeves), who unlocks the secret of the matrix and is able to ultimately defeat the computer control of all humanity. His revolutionary act, which reaches its end point in the third volume *The Matrix Revolutions* (Lana and Lilly Wachowski, 2003), provides a potential model for emancipation that has had incredible theoretical resonance. From Alain Badiou and Cornel West to David Chalmers and Daniel Dennett, thinkers of many different stripes have taken *The Matrix* as philosophically or politically paradigmatic.[3]

Amid the acclaim for *The Matrix*, Josef Rusnak's *The Thirteenth Floor* (1999) slipped under the theoretical radar. Rusnak's film lacked the budget and stars of *The Matrix*, but it had the virtue of providing a political structure more attuned to the form of emancipatory enjoyment than its richer counterpart. The similarities between the two films are obvious: both involve characters caught up in simulated realities from which they must try to emancipate themselves—and in the process carve out some freedom for themselves. But the differences are even more significant. Neo achieves his initial emancipation in *The Matrix* through the recognition that nothing that he encounters is actually real. When he fully recognizes the unreality of everything he encounters, he gains the ability to manipulate the world of the matrix in order to defeat the computer's agents and eventually (in the third film) lead humanity to a collective emancipation from its oppressed condition. In *The Thirteenth Floor*, in contrast, hero Douglas Hall (Craig Bierko) must immerse himself in the manipulation and encounter its internal contradiction in order to discover the possibility of

---

Michell's *Notting Hill*, Steven Soderbergh's *The Limey*, Doug Liman's *Go*, Alexander Payne's *Election*, Pedro Almodóvar's *All About My Mother*, Spike Jonze's *Being John Malkovich*, Anthony Minghella's *The Talented Mr. Ripley*, Jim Jarmusch's *Ghost Dog*, and Kimberly Peirce's *Boys Don't Cry*.

3   See, for instance, Alain Badiou et al., *Matrix: Machine philosophique* (Paris: Ellipses, 2013).

emancipation. By bringing the hero to a confrontation with the contradiction that defines his social order, this film gives us a sense of what emancipatory enjoyment looks like.

The Matrix presents the political act as occurring through the ability to recognize that reality is faked, that it is the result of an ideological manipulation. Armed with the conviction that nothing he sees is real, Neo can ultimately defeat the matrix and its various defenders. When he gains sufficient distance from the illusion of the images that surround him, he begins to see the symbolic code itself rather than the imaginary plenitude that this code subtends. Unlike the other people operating within the matrix, he escapes being duped by the fullness of what he sees through his ability to achieve psychic distance from the visual field of images. He reads the code rather than being impressed by the images. As a result, he can act freely within the coded reality and even defeat the power of the computers outside of the symbolic reality. According to the logic of the film, the political act consists in seeing through the power of ideology by stepping back from it and recognizing its falsity. Neo serves as a political model that succeeds through withdrawal and knowledge. He is the one because he can accede to the proper level of consciousness.

Unlike *The Matrix*, the *Thirteenth Floor* does not paint the path to truth as taking a step back from our ideologically slanted reality. Here one must proceed even further—fully—into the deception to discover and embrace the contradiction within the social order. Only in this direction is a genuinely emancipatory position possible, according to the wager of the film. Rather than recognizing the deceptiveness of the ideological illusion, one must initially fall for it in order to discover its point of contradiction, which is the point where the social order opens up to the outside. One achieves the enjoyment of transcendence not by stepping back but by pushing forward to the fundamental social contradiction and inhabiting that contradiction. The key difference between *The Matrix* and *The Thirteenth Floor* lies in how each film conceives the political act. *The Thirteenth Floor* shows how one might occupy the point of contradiction in order to attain a radical political enjoyment and emancipation.

The Thirteenth Floor begins within a fantasy world—a computer simulation of Los Angeles in the 1930s—created by Hannon Fuller (Armin Mueller-Stahl) and Douglas Hall. In the persona of his identity within the simulation, Fuller writes a note to Douglas, and his voiceover reveals its contents. He says, "They say, 'ignorance is bliss.' For the first time in my life, I agree. I wish I had never uncovered the awful truth." The voiceover stops before Fuller offers an explanation of "the awful truth" (though he includes this explanation in the note that Douglas will later read), and someone murders him just after he leaves the simulated world. Consequently, the spectator begins the film with a hint about some "awful truth" but without any idea concerning the content of this truth. But Fuller's voiceover offers an indication something is not quite right in the structure of the filmic reality. The truth that Fuller has discovered turns out to be the unreality of his own reality. Fuller discovers that what Douglas and he took for reality—their shared world of experience—is itself a simulation functioning just like the simulation that they have created within their world. He recognizes that their world is an ideological construct, the created product of some external agency, which implies that Fuller, Douglas, and everyone within their world lacks the freedom that they thought they had. This discovery of the unreality of his reality and the unfreedom of his freedom represents an "awful truth" for Fuller because it undermines his belonging to the world, his sense of where he is.

Fuller arrives at this truth not through the kind of distance from the deception that Morpheus (Lawrence Fishburne) helps Neo to employ in *The Matrix*, but through immersing himself in the fantasy world of the computer simulation. In *The Matrix*, the computer simulation (the matrix created by the machines who rule the earth) disguises what is real and represents the barrier that Neo must overcome in order to experience this real; in *The Thirteenth Floor*, the simulation provides the vehicle Fuller (and later, Douglas) uses to encounter the contradiction that exposes the ideological manipulation.

Though Fuller dies before he can communicate his encounter with the world's limits to Douglas, Douglas eventually learns of it through the hotel bartender from the simulation, Jerry Ashton (Vincent D'Onofrio), to whom Fuller left his note for Douglas. When Ashton initially tells Douglas about the letter, Douglas believes that Fuller was describing the simulation that they created, and this confuses him. He asks himself, "Why would Fuller write to me about the limitations of the simulation? I know the limitations." Soon, however, Douglas recognizes that the point of the letter was to inform him that his own reality—the reality he inhabits with Fuller and out of which they created the simulation—was also a simulation. Douglas drives to the point where the consistency of his world breaks down, a point where the film reveals visually what one sees at the edge of the symbolic structure.

After Douglas begins to suspect the truth, we see a series of shots depicting him driving out of Los Angeles. When he finally arrives at the edge of his (simulated) reality, the film initially offers an objective shot of Douglas looking. A reverse long shot from behind Douglas follows this objective shot of his face looking, and the long shot shows us what Douglas sees. In this shot, we see the normal reality of Douglas's filmic world blend into a matrix of intersecting green lines, lines that seem to provide the underlying symbolic structure for the world. This image of the barrier of the symbolic reality appears only briefly in two shots that the film intersperses with shots of Douglas looking. When Douglas's cellular phone rings during the last of these shots, his subsequent conversation with Jane Fuller (Gretchen Mol), Hannon Fuller's daughter, reveals his understanding of what he sees. He tells her, "I know the truth." Jane Fuller responds, "Where are you?" And Douglas answers, "You could say it's the end of the world." After the film cuts away from Douglas's discovery of the end of the world, the effect of this encounter with the real immediately registers a disturbance in the form of the film.

An establishing shot of Los Angeles indicates Douglas's return to the city to meet with Jane Fuller, but two quick jump cuts interrupt this standard establishing shot. The jump cuts indicate the disturbance in the symbolic structure of the film—an effect of this encounter with the contradictory point at the limit of his world. The encounter reveals to Douglas—and to the spectator— the inconsistent and incomplete nature of his symbolic world. He comes to occupy the point where the world begins—a contradictory point where the world both is and isn't. It is a point of impossibility where the world loses its consistency. While this encounter is traumatic for Douglas, it also enables him to transcend his world, to inhabit an impossible site that doesn't exist on the map of his world. As a result, this act frees him from that world's power over him, even as it horrifies him with the revelation of his own simulated status. On the basis of this experience of transcendence, Douglas becomes free of his investment in his own symbolic world because he goes beyond its confines. The encounter with the point of contradiction condemns Douglas and the spectator to occupy this point of transcendence.

The Thirteenth Floor shows the relation that the emancipatory project must adopt toward contradiction. Embracing the contradiction is the path to a liberating enjoyment. This enjoyment occurs within the failures of the social order. Even though only Douglas experiences it in the film, it is available to everyone. Everyone can drive to the end of the world and confront its contradictory end point because manifestations of this contradictory point are everywhere. By doing so, one accesses the universality of a failure that holds everyone together. This is the source of an enjoyment that emancipates, the enjoyment of nonbelonging. When faced with the coordinates of the social order laid bare, individuals see and experience their nonbelonging and recognize that their nonbelonging is also everyone's nonbelonging.

11.

Keep Your
Friends Close

CONSERVATIVE ENJOYMENT IS ALWAYS derivative. It translates the emancipatory enjoyment of an internal contradiction into the enjoyment of an opposition, the opposition between the friend and the enemy, between those who belong and those who don't. The internal contradiction is always primary to this opposition, which means that the leftist form of enjoyment also has primacy relative to the rightist form. Every social order has a fundamental internal contradiction that plays a constitutive role in that order and in the way that the order structures enjoyment. Although the enjoyment transcends what the social order allows as possible, it nonetheless emerges out of the contradiction that defines the order.

The enemy that the rightist forges out of the contradiction is always a stand-in for the inherent failure of the social order itself. The enemy emerges as the personification of the contradiction, a personification that makes the path to enjoyment clearer for the rightist than for the leftist, even though right-wing enjoyment represents a fundamental betrayal of the basic emancipatory possibility inherent in the social structure. The threat that the enemy poses to the existing order is a formal requirement of the rightist conception of the political terrain, not anything inherent within the enemy itself. The enemy might be initially innocuous and become a threat only because the regime considers it to be one. The enemy could also be a serious threat. But most often, the Right props up an enemy, at least in its internal version, that bears no threat at all. This is the case, for example, with immigrants in contemporary Europe. In this instance, the attempt to fantasize a threat into existence comes up woefully short. The vehemence of the attack on the internal enemy corresponds to the absence of any real threat that it poses to the existing regime.

Carl Schmitt explains the rightist structure of enjoyment in his attempt to define politics as such. He doesn't think that his definition of politics is confined to the Right and not all-encompassing because Schmitt cannot imagine a world without enemies. This is how we know that he is a right-wing thinker, if the historical evidence of his membership in the Nazi Party is not enough to convince us. But Schmitt doesn't simply argue for the existence of an enemy to act as a target for all a people's aggression. He has a theoretical justification for the enemy that even takes into account the problems raised by capitalist society.

According to Schmitt, having an enemy is essential to the creation of a public sphere. Without an enemy, modern capitalist subjects confine themselves to the realm of privacy and never recognize their bond with others. In *The Concept of the Political*, he argues for the importance of the distinction between friend and enemy. The enemy is a political necessity, a condition for the political field. He claims, "The enemy is solely the public enemy, because everything that has a relationship to such a collectivity of men, particularly to a whole nation, becomes public by virtue of such a relationship."[1] As Schmitt sees it, we can only come together as a coherent group when confronted by an enemy that gives us a common target for our violent impulses. Otherwise, we remain private beings who treat our fellow citizens aggressively without any sense of a social bond holding us together.[2] Better an exter-

---

1   Carl Schmitt, *The Concept of the Political*, trans. George Schwab (Chicago: University of Chicago Press, 1996), 28.

2   If one reads *The Concept of the Political* attentively, but for his apotheosis of war, Schmitt sounds conspicuously like leftist critics of capitalism. It is thus

nal enemy to hate than ceaseless internal strife. What Schmitt doesn't see but implicitly acknowledges with this theory is that the internal strife—the society's internal contradiction—has priority over the formation of the enemy. We create the opposition to the enemy in order to retreat from the enjoyment that the society's internal contradiction offers.

Despite Schmitt's connection to Nazism, it is clear that he has a point. Anyone who has lived through a war or through warlike relations with another nation can testify to the bonding power that this has for one's country. But what he misses—and what conservatism as a philosophy misses—is the deleterious effect that the enemy has on politics. Instead of giving birth to political struggle, as Schmitt erroneously claims, the erection of an enemy represents the death knell of politics.

Nothing produces domestic consensus as much as a war. One's neighbors, even those with whom one has vehement political disagreements, become tolerable. Such consensus is not the expression of politics but the mark of its absence. War with an external enemy smothers internal political contestation with the agreement that one must be united against the common foe. Internal consensus is not just a typical reaction to war but the ubiquitous one. The declaration of war or even the naming of an external enemy always props up the ruling party at the expense of any other political vision. To oppose the ruling party is to risk the charge of giving aid and comfort to the enemy. Political opposition

---

perfectly understandable why leftists such as Chantal Mouffe have found an important resource in his thought. He sees the gated community of the typical bourgeois as the nadir of human existence. He writes, "The bourgeois is an individual who does not want to leave the apolitical riskless private sphere. He rests in the possession of his private property, and under the justification of his possessive individualism he acts as an individual against the totality." Carl Schmitt, *The Concept of the Political*, 62. By invoking the concern of the totality against the private individual, Schmitt reveals his hostility to the logic of capital, albeit from the Right rather than from the Left.

becomes treason in times of war. Consensus or the absence of politics becomes synonymous with patriotism.

This is why it is impossible to follow Schmitt down the path of crediting the enemy with constituting the political field. He writes, "The high points of politics are simultaneously the moments in which the enemy is, in concrete clarity, recognized as the enemy."[3] Despite his professed desire to preserve the political field of contestation against the fall into consensus, what Schmitt really wants in his call for an enemy is to tilt the political field to the Right. The external enemy turns the political struggle around internal contradiction into an apolitical opposition.

For the Right, the enemy is not simply an external threat, like the Soviet Union was for the United States during the Cold War. In order to mobilize the enjoyment that derives from the social order's internal contradiction, the external enemy must correspond to an enemy within. This is why the battle of the Cold War required enemy communists within the United States that conservative political figures could sniff out. It was not enough to battle the Soviet Union. One also had to battle such innocuous figures as left-leaning actors Sterling Hayden and Edward G. Robinson.

By figuring the enemy as an internal threat, the rightist brings the opposition of friend and enemy closer to the contradiction that defines the Left. In this sense, Senator Joseph McCarthy is more proximate to Toussaint Louverture than a moderate leader like Tony Blair is. Through his paranoid search for communists everywhere within the American power establishment, McCarthy revealed the distinction between friend and enemy as internal to the American political order, which is not totally removed from Toussaint Louverture identifying the contradiction within the colonialist policies of revolutionary France. Although McCarthy requires an enemy in a way that Toussaint Louverture does not, the status of the enemy—politically harmless screenwriters and

---

3   Carl Schmitt, *The Concept of the Political*, 67.

actors—illustrates that American capitalism produces its own op-position, even if McCarthy could not avow this himself, which is why he remained a conservative and did not become a leftist like Toussaint Louverture.

For the conservative to continue to enjoy, the enemy must remain a constant threat. There is no moment of peace for this en-joying structure, no interval between the dissipation of one ene-my and the erection of another. When the Soviet Union collapses, the West quickly turns to Islamicist terror as the new enemy. In order for enjoyment of secular capitalist society to remain possi-ble, it must have an enemy that seeks to destroy it. This enemy is the source of its enjoyability.

The anti-immigrant right-wing populist leader shows nicely that the only enjoyment is the enjoyment of nonbelonging. Al-though the right-wing populist leader stresses the need to keep immigrants out in order to facilitate the nation continuing to en-joy itself, this enjoyment that the leader arouses in nationalist fol-lowers exists only through the image of the threat that immigrants pose to the enjoyment of those who belong. Those who are in can only enjoy by identifying with those who are outside, even while they pour their hatred onto these figures. There is no reactionary enjoyment that doesn't emerge in those it vilifies.

In the midterm election of 2018, Donald Trump illustrated this logic perfectly. Faced with the prospect of dramatic losses for his party in Congress, Trump began to warn about a caravan of migrants headed for the southern border of the United States. According to his rhetoric, this caravan was tantamount to an in-vasion, a threat that required sending the military to the border in order to repel the oncoming horde. But immediately after the election, all concern about the caravan dissipated. Trump no lon-ger spoke of it. Its sole purpose was to arouse potential conserva-tive voters enough that they would vote rather than just staying home. Faced with an electoral crisis, Trump had no other recourse for arousal than appealing to the imminent threat of immigrants. The enjoyment of these would-be immigrants became the vehicle for arousing that of his followers. This is not an exceptional tactic but the only possible one for the right-wing leader. The enemy must have a privileged position in the conservative structure because the outsider's enjoyment has the effect of constituting that of the people who try to belong to the society.

One would think that the derivative nature of rightist enjoyment would put conservatives at a political disadvantage. But it turns out that enjoying through one's enemy is a psychically easier prospect than avowing enjoyment as one's own. Enjoying through the enemy enables one to disavow the enjoyment, to imagine oneself without the obscenity of enjoyment that one attributes to the outsider. Finding their own enjoyment in the other enables people to remain pure, at least in their conscious thinking, from the stain of this enjoyment. Thus, despite appearances, the existence of an enemy gives the Right an inherent enjoyment advantage over the Left. It is psychically easier to adhere to the Right rather than the Left because a genuine leftism forces the subject to see itself as part of the problem. Confronting an enemy is always less difficult than enduring one's own internal contradiction.

The enemy creates the illusion of belonging for those who aren't this enemy. Symbolic identity becomes constituted through those who don't belong. The enemy figure of nonbelonging—like the Jew in Nazi Germany or the communist in the Indonesia of the late 1990s or the immigrant in contemporary Europe—allows others to believe that they belong. What they cannot recognize is that their belonging is always faked because it is actually dependent on those who don't belong. The enjoyment of an identity comes from the outsider who appears to pose a threat to that identity.

12.

Father Christmas

EVERY POLITICAL REGIME, WHETHER Right or Left, requires someone or some group ultimately to make the decisions. The Right has no problem with this necessity since the conservative political structure must have an exception in order to create the group. The exception is the leader. Right-wing thinking depends on an exception who inherently occupies the position to rule. This thinking establishes a hierarchical relationship between the leader and the people, so that the leader can easily take up a position above everyone else. This is why there are numerous examples of successful rightist leaders who led regimes that were not especially oppressive. From Winston Churchill to Charles de Gaulle to Angela Merkel, it is not difficult to enumerate instances of successful conservative governance. There are also much more brutal right-wing leaders who managed to rule according to extreme rightist principles for a long time, such as Francisco Franco in Spain or Augusto Pinochet in Chile. All of these leaders governed as exceptions. Their exceptional status relative to the social order gave a justification and credibility to their rule. The figure of the leader qua exception derives from the rightist conception of the political field. As an exception, the leader creates an opening for people's enjoyment, which is a possibility that doesn't exist in an emancipatory structure.

The situation for the Left is entirely different. In an emancipatory regime, the leader cannot be an exception to the rule that governs everyone else. Such a hierarchy would give the lie to the idea of emancipation, which must be egalitarian if it is to be emancipatory. Once leftist leaders become exceptions, they cease to be leftist leaders and turn into their opposite number. Thus, it is almost impossible to name leftist leaders who have had a sustained period of success. Typically, they are either quickly deposed, like Toussaint Louverture, or they begin to follow the rightist path after being in power for too long, like Jean-Jacques Dessalines, the leader who took over for the deceased Toussaint Louverture in Haiti. Maximilien Robespierre took both of these seemingly contradictory paths. He transformed from a zealot against the death penalty and foreign wars into a proponent of both, and then the more conservative members of the French Revolution cut short his time in power by making him significantly shorter.[1] The brevity of Robespierre's position as the primary leader of the French government is not at all unusual. Leftist leadership is always problematic.

The leftist leader must rule without becoming an exception. Figures who are able to do so are difficult to find. One must look to someone such as Evo Morales for the paradigm of the left-wing leader, although even his rule ended with a reactionary coup. Other than Morales, models of emancipatory leaders in power are incredibly scarce. As a result, we must resort to looking for them in one of the least obvious places—the Hollywood Christmas film.

The Christmas film seems like the most ideological product that Hollywood generates. Following almost exactly the paradigm of capitalist accumulation, this type of film typically recounts a series of disappointments that the hero overcomes on the way to the perfect enjoyment that Christmas day brings. Just as one receives commodities on Christmas day, Christmas functions in these films like the perfect commodity, relieving the subject from its lack and bringing forth an unbridled satisfaction. From *It's a Wonderful Life* (Frank Capra, 1946) and *Miracle on 34th Street*

---

1   That is, Robespierre was guillotined.

(George Seaton, 1947) to *Die Hard* (John McTiernan, 1988) and *Christmas Vacation* (Jeremiah Chechik, 1989), the Christmas film depicts a trajectory from lack to plenitude that characterizes capitalist ideology. There appears to be little doubt about the fundamental political conservatism of this genre of film.

But something unexpected almost always happens on the path to the plenitude of Christmas day in these films. In other words, the enjoyment does not lie where one might expect it to. Instead, it is almost invariably produced through the symbolic castration of the father figure. This is a staple of the Christmas film, an unexpected requirement of the genre. The Christmas film succeeds in generating enjoyment only as a result of the father's failure, and it is this failure that opens the space for the enjoyment that emerges in the film. Just as the emergence of Christ announces God becoming human and taking the form of a lacking subject, the Christmas movie reveals the lack in the father figure.[2] To enjoy a Christmas film is to enjoy the failed father. Rather than being an exception, the leader's failure is the source of the bond.

This is politically significant because grasping the leader as a failed father—as a figure who suffers from lack just like everyone else—is the key to emancipation. Structuring the social order around a leader who is structurally distinct but not socially distinct is what gives a society an egalitarian hue. As long as the leader or leaders remain exceptions apart from the rest of society, the society will produce a conservative form of enjoyment in which some must be excluded so that others can belong. The Christmas film shows a social organization forming around a figure who

---

2   Even though the actual practice of Christianity almost always fails to achieve the grandeur of Hegel's conception of it that views it as the religion of God's castration, the makers of Christmas films almost always appear to have read Hegel when they approach Christianity. For Hegel, the God of the beyond shows himself to be a finite figure of humiliation when he fully appears. The appearance of Christ is the humiliation of the God of the beyond. Likewise, in the Christmas film, the symbolic father's castration is a generic requirement.

structures the social organization despite his evident castration. The father is here just a formal position, not a content, as the leader must be in an emancipated society.

We can see this same structure in almost every version of the Christmas film, but Ernst Lubitsch's *The Shop Around the Corner* establishes the pattern in 1940. Lubitsch's Christmas movie shows the budding romance of two coworkers at Matuschek and Company, a retail shop specializing in leather goods in Budapest. Alfred Kralik (James Stewart) and Klara Novak (Margaret Sullavan) develop an epistolary relationship without each realizing that they are corresponding with a coworker. The film ends with the revelation that the two coworkers who constantly bicker with each other are the letter writers, which prompts them to embark on an actual romance. But as it depicts the flowering romance between Kralik and Novak, *The Shop Around the Corner* also shows the collapse of the father figure, the owner of the shop, Hugo Matuschek (Frank Morgan). Discovering his wife's infidelity with a worker at the shop, Matuschek tries to kill himself. After his release from the hospital, Matuschek visits the shop on Christmas Eve, where he sees record-breaking sales.

Despite the shop's success, Matuschek appears as a broken man due to the infidelity and suicide attempt. He pathetically asks various coworkers to join him for a Christmas dinner, but everyone already has plans, including even the former errand boy Pepi (William Tracy). Finally, Matuschek is able to convince the newly hired young errand boy, Rudy (Charles Smith), to join him, but this underscores rather than eliminates the pathos that engulfs him at this moment. Matuschek's isolation and his status as a cuckhold are not incidental to the filmic narrative but provide the key to the enjoyment of this narrative.

Typically, the father figure functions as the force for exclusion. He patrols the barrier between belonging and nonbelonging, making sure that this barrier remains secure. In this sense, the father figure is central to the project of right-wing enjoyment. His potency expels the enemy and thereby secures rightist enjoyment. Without the nonlacking father figure who has what it takes to keep the riff raff out, this form of enjoyment has no way to keep the enemy at bay and could not sustain itself. The castrated father of the Christmas film cannot perform the function that the conservative form of enjoyment requires, which is what gives these films their radical hue, in spite of their apparent investment in the day where the worship of the commodity reaches its apex.[3]

The conclusion of *The Shop Around the Corner* does depict the exclusion of Vadas (Joseph Schildkraut), who had the affair with Matuschek's wife. But this exclusion is not the source of the enjoyment that the film produces. Vadas doesn't function as an enemy providing a way for the spectator to enjoy. Even though he cuckholds Matuschek, it is not the father figure who fires him but Kralik. The film presents Vadas as a comic figure rather than as a villain. The enjoyment produced in the film circulates around Matuschek's absence, not Vadas's expulsion.

In *The Shop Around the Corner*, the failure of the father figure allows a collective to form on the basis of his lack. We see this occur when the workers at Matuschek and Company come together to work on Christmas Eve. Matuschek's absence is the site of the bond among the employees, the point through which they collectively enjoy. This structuring absence, the result of the father's evident lack, facilitates the connection between the workers that

---

3   In the underrated *Christmas in Connecticut* (Peter Godfrey, 1945), magazine magnate Alexander Yardley (Sydney Greenstreet) displays a total control that doesn't even allow others to speak their defiance of his plans. As a result, he always gets what he wants. But as the action of the film unfurls, the romance between Elizabeth Lane (Barbara Stanwyck) and Jefferson Jones (Dennis Morgan) thwarts his designs. The lovers come together in spite of his intimidation and threats that attempt to keep them apart. Yardley's attempt to put a stop to the romance does nothing but reveal his own impotence as a symbolic father.

did not exist while he was at the store. The father figure guards the barrier that creates belonging and hides collective nonbelonging. His failure and absence render this collective nonbelonging visible and create the possibility for a collective enjoyment of it.[4]

In Christmas comedies, the enjoyment of the father figure's failure is even more pronounced. The comedy in these films centers on the father's inadequacy. *Christmas Vacation* finds much of its humor in the failures of Clark Griswold (Chevy Chase), the film's father figure. Clark attempts several ambitious projects for Christmas, such as chopping down a tree in the wild and illuminating the family house with thousands of lights. Each of these projects goes awry because of Clark's own comic inadequacy. His effort to light the house initially fails because he doesn't turn on the outlet where all the lights are plugged in. When he prepares the family to see the house brightly lit, he produces nothing at all. The lights come on later when a houseguest flips a light switch in the garage, but then they go out just as quickly when she flips the switch off. The lighting is so extreme that when they do illuminate for this brief interval, power goes off around the neighborhood. Even when the lighting works, something goes awry. Clark's inability to light the house properly provides the point of enjoyment for the spectator.

The lighting fiasco is at the center of the comedy in *Christmas Vacation*. Clark's initial failure is itself humorous, especially when it becomes apparent that the failure is the result of simply forgetting to flip a light switch. The fact that he checked each of the thousands of bulbs individually makes the simplicity of the solution even more comic. When the lights do come on, the film cuts to Clark's neighbors, who are lying together on their bed in

---

4   The remake of *The Shop Around the Corner*, *You've Got Mail* (Nora Ephron, 1998), is not a total failure. It actually adds a critique of predatory capitalism that is absent in its forerunner. But what it lacks is the figure of the castrated father. This limits the remake's radicality in relation to the Lubitsch original.

their dimly lit bedroom. The magnitude of the brightness is so extreme that it temporarily blinds these neighbors. At the moment when they stand to close their curtains, the lights go off and leave them falling in the dark. A few moments later, Clark's spouse Ellen (Beverly D'Angelo) flips the light switch again. The lights come on and once more blind the neighbors, causing one of them to fall down the stairs while carrying a tray with dishes. This pratfall is comic because of the role that Clark's ineptitude has in causing it. The saga of the Griswold Christmas lights shows the castrated father as the site of enjoyment in the film. Clark's incessant failures constitute the comedy of *Christmas Vacation* and show how the father's castration creates a point at which we enjoy absence.

Through its emphasis on the castration of the father figure, the Christmas film locates enjoyment in the moment of failure. At the point where the father fails, the collective enjoys. Without this figure policing the barrier between belonging and nonbelonging, it becomes possible to enjoy nonbelonging, to enjoy through absence rather than through the promise of presence. Despite the sentimentality of the Christmas film, this genre's depiction of the father's failure situates it clearly on the side of leftist politics. The Christmas film shows the way that the Left can fight against its inherent enjoyment disadvantage. By showing enjoyment through the father's failure, this type of film indicates that absence can be even more enjoyable than having an enemy.

If we want to envision what emancipatory institutions look like, we should look to the Christmas film with its depiction of the castrated father figure. By organizing social formations around such figures, these films show us how to construct a society of nonbelonging. There is no enemy, and no one experiences the illusory privilege of belonging. Instead, everyone comes together around what's missing—the authority of the father. This absence facilitates their enjoyment rather than detracting from it. In this way, the Christmas film functions as a paradigmatic genre for the Left.

In the struggle between competing forms of enjoyment, the structural advantages of the Right are clear. But leftist enjoyment has an authenticity that the right-wing alternative doesn't have. Rightist enjoyment is always parasitical on that of the Left. It enjoys through exclusion, but it partakes in the enjoyment of non-belonging in those excluded. Its exclusivity depends on obscuring the source of the enjoyment it provides because this source is nonbelonging itself. Rightist enjoyment requires the enemy that it attacks, whereas leftism finds its enjoyment in its own contradiction. The leftist doesn't need an enemy because it has itself.

13

The Safety
of the Superego

THE LEFT ATTACKS ITSELF rather than an enemy, which is always the target of the Right. But the Left's self-critique derails when it becomes superegoic—that is, when it singles out traitors to the cause of emancipation for their failure to be pure enough. The turn to the superego represents the fundamental way that the project of emancipation goes awry. Superegoic moralism is a leftist self-critique that ceases to be concerned with achieving emancipation and instead focuses on striving toward moral purity. With the turn to the superego, the emancipatory project undergoes a woeful transformation: a political struggle becomes a moral one.

Under the constraint of the superego, emancipation gives way to a constant pressure to prove one's moral bona fides. Instead of insisting on the enjoyment of contradiction that derives from nonbelonging, the superego pushes the Left to create belonging through the elimination of any impurities. It attempts to purge those statements and thoughts that evince any investment in social hierarchy. The turn to the superego represents a masochistic attack on leftists for coming up short in the effort to rid themselves of oppressive thoughts, language, and actions. Superegoic politics is inherently self-defeating because it leaves no one standing. There is no pure subject that can withstand the rigors of the superego's assault, since it concerns itself not just with what one does but also with what one thinks.[1]

The turn to superegoic moralism marks the retreat from a genuine leftism to the promise of belonging for those who don't belong. Even though this moralism presents itself as the most radical position imaginable, it remains firmly on the terrain of belonging, which is the terrain of the right. Under the pressure of the superego, nonbelonging transforms into a new form of belonging. The authority of the superego polices the border of this new belonging in order to ensure that no one transgresses it. Any acquiescence to the logic of the enemy, any transgression of the proper language, results in a superegoic assault. Violating the dictates of ideological correctness leaves the transgressor at the mercy of an authority's imperative.

The superego is the internalization of social authority. Although we tend to associate the superego with an impetus to act morally—it is often pictured as the angel on one of our shoulders, opposed by the devilish id on the other—it is not an agency of morality at all.[2] It pressures us to obey the voice of authority, most

---

1   In his theorization of the superego, Freud makes clear why it is so exacting. As a social and psychic agency, the superego leaves no stone unturned. There is no place in the psyche where the subject has respite from its probing. As Freud points out in *Civilization and Its Discontents*, "nothing can be hidden from the super-ego, not even thoughts." Sigmund Freud, *Civilization and Its Discontents*, trans. James Strachey, in *The Standard Edition of the Complete Psychological Works of Sigmund Freud*, ed. James Strachey (London: Hogarth, 1961), 21:125. Because it sees everywhere, the superego recognizes the necessary impurity of the subject's thoughts. This is the source of our inability ever to satisfy its demands.

2   Mladen Dolar insists on the stark difference between the superego and the moral law. In *A Voice and Nothing More*, he states, "the voice of the superego is not the voice of reason but, rather, the voice of reason run amok, reason berserk. The superego is not the moral law, despite Freud's declarations to the contrary, but a way of eluding it." Mladen Dolar, *A Voice and Nothing More* (Cambridge: MIT Press, 2006), 99. Kant's moral law functions as an imperative for the subject, but, in contrast to the superego, it does not derive

often in a way that transgresses the official laws of the society in favor of its unwritten rules.[3] The superego says, "You must obey." But this command comes with a catch: no amount of obedience is ever enough to satiate the superegoic demand. This failure to obey has the effect of creating a libidinal attachment to the figure of authority. The point of the superego is not to generate moral action but to drive the subject into a state of total dependence on the commands of the authority.

In *Moses and Monotheism*, Freud provides one of his most helpful accounts of how the logic of the superego functions. He states, "It keeps the ego in a permanent state of dependence and exercises a constant pressure on it. Just as in childhood, the ego is apprehensive about risking the love of its supreme master; it feels his approval as liberation and satisfaction and his reproaches as pangs of conscience."[4] In response to superegoic pressure, one attempts to obey, to answer the superego's call, but one can never obey enough. The failure to be adequate to the superego's demand is written into that demand. This failure doesn't break the bond with the social authority but cements it. To give in to the superego is to find oneself completely at the mercy of the social authority.

It is impossible to heed its demand adequately. The more that one gives in to the pressure of the superego, the more that the

---

from the social authority. The Kantian moral law gives us freedom from the demands of the social authority, which is why Dolar claims that Freud's condemnation of the Kantian moral law is superegoic.

3 Slavoj Žižek's most important contribution to understanding conservative social cohesion is his insistence that the bond that unites a conservative group is a shared transgression, not the official laws that publicly articulate the social link. According to Žižek, the shared transgression allows for a connection that exists only among those in the know and inherently excludes outsiders who know only the public laws.

4 Sigmund Freud, *Moses and Monotheism*, trans. James Strachey, in *The Standard Edition of the Complete Psychological Works of Sigmund Freud*, ed. James Strachey (London: Hogarth Press, 1964), 23:117.

superego demands that one give.[5] This is how we can see when the superego is activated: if obedience triggers an increased demand for more obedience, then we are trapped within the superegoic predicament with no possible escape. Under the pressure of the superego, one must constantly prove one's bona fides, but no act can successfully accomplish this.

The turn to the superego actually represents the Left's abandonment of its form of enjoyment. It causes us to give up enjoyment not by enforcing moral restrictions but paradoxically through an imperative of enjoyment. In his radical reinterpretation of the superego, Jacques Lacan associates it not with restrictions on enjoyment but with the command to enjoy. In his *Seminar XX*, he states, "Nothing forces anyone to enjoy except the superego. The superego is the imperative of jouissance—Enjoy!"[6] The problem is that the imperative to enjoy is the surest way to bar enjoyment, just like telling myself that I must go to sleep is the way to ensure a sleepless night. Enjoyment can come only as a by-product. The superego pressures the subject to enjoy and thereby forces the subject to confront incessantly its failure to enjoy.

---

5   In his most thorough theorization of superegoic pressure (which occurs in *The Metastases of Enjoyment*), Slavoj Žižek accounts for the connection between capitulation to the social authority and the unquenchable demand of the superego. He writes, "superego draws the energy of the pressure it exerts on the subject from the fact that the subject was not faithful to his desire, that he gave it up. Our sacrificing to the superego, our paying tribute to it, only corroborates our guilt. For that reason our debt to the superego is unredeemable: the more we pay it off, the more we owe. Superego is like the extortioner slowly bleeding us to death—the more he gets, the stronger his hold on us." Slavoj Žižek, *The Metastases of Enjoyment: Six Essays on Women and Causality* (London: Verso, 1994), 68. Our compliance is never enough because it receives its energy from every betrayal of our desire for the sake of the social demand. The more we comply, the more we abandon the desire that pushes us away from capitulation.

6   Jacques Lacan, *The Seminar of Jacques Lacan, Book XX: Encore 1972–1973*, trans. Bruce Fink, ed. Jacques-Alain Miller (New York: Norton, 1998), 3.

Superegoic pressure to enjoy on the Left becomes most explicit in one of the famous slogans from May 1968 in Paris. On the walls around Paris one could read *Jouir sans entraves*—"Enjoy without hindrances." With this imperative, we can see Lacan's definition of the superegoic imperative to enjoy written out literally. One must not only enjoy but must do so without any limits whatsoever. While this seems an extreme version of leftist superegoism, it actually makes evident exactly how the superego always operates and why no one can successfully obey its imperatives. The attempt to enjoy without limits is doomed to failure because the source of our enjoyment is the limit.

This becomes clear if we think of any enjoyable experience. An ice cream cone provides more enjoyment than having an unlimited vat of ice cream to eat. A walk through the Badlands is enjoyable, but living one's entire life there would not be. One enjoys a tennis match that lasts only two hours but not one that lasts two days. In each case, the limit is constitutive of the enjoyment because one enjoys through the limit, not *sans entraves*.

The turn to the superego and its moralizing condemnation is always a temptation for emancipatory politics. Engaging in superegoic moralizing has a clear appeal because it brings quicker results than political engagement. We can target political actors or those in the public eye who take up objectionable positions and work to eliminate them and their views from the public sphere. By doing so, we make the public sphere more egalitarian and more accessible to those who have previously been denied access to it.

Today we are witnessing the rise of a superegoic turn on the Left. It manifests itself in the preoccupation with purity among political actors and anyone in the public eye. The superego targets any impurities, any points at which the subject has taken the side of power rather than that of the powerless. Superegoic leftism attempts to produce an egalitarian society by cleansing the people that would constitute this society. If people cease to have prejudiced views, they will usher in a new egalitarian social structure, so the logic of superegoic leftism goes.

The Left, of course, does not have a monopoly on recourse to the superego. But the superego takes on dramatically different forms for the Right and the Left. The far-right zealot is typically a superegoic figure who demands that followers transgress social mores and engage in violent destructiveness in the name of devotion to the leader's authority. This is clearly evident in the outbursts of political violence among Hitler's SA (*Sturmabteilung*) that came to a head during *Kristallnacht* (the Night of Broken Glass), when the SA destroyed thousands of Jewish-owned buildings and synagogues, while killing nearly a hundred Jews. The activity of *Kristallnacht*, despite its rampant immorality, bears all the markings of superegoic pressure. The SA carried out this destruction in an effort to evince their obedience to the authority of the leader. The right-wing superego typically has a high body count. It manifests itself in events such as *Kristallnacht*, lynchings, and hooliganism.

While the rightist turn to the superego causes more explicit destruction, when the Left follows this path, it loses its way altogether. A superegoic Right destroys its enemies, but a superegoic Left ends up eating itself, precisely at the time when it should emphasize its universalist claims. The pressure of the superego is such that no one can ultimately pass its test. The one invoking its claim today will succumb to it tomorrow.

What's most destructive about the leftist turn to the superego is that it doesn't further the aim that it purportedly seeks. The pressure of the superego doesn't eliminate outbursts of racism, sexism, homophobia, and transphobia. It exacerbates them. The more one feels superegoic pressure rather than the freedom of a political project, the more one succumbs to what one tries to avoid. Superegoic moralism is a way of avoiding emancipatory politics, not engaging in it.[7]

---

7   Superegoic moralism never turns its attention to the exigencies of the capitalist economy. It lets capitalism off the hook because the manifestations of its destructiveness do not clearly violate moral injunctions. The exploitation of workers in Indonesia that enables one to buy an inexpensive pair of jeans is not visible in the jeans, whereas the homophobic slur that someone utters is perceptible. The superego gives the violence of capitalism a pass because it seems unconnected to any individual actors. And yet, capitalism represents the foundation of contemporary oppression.

14.

Let a Hundred
Trotskys Bloom

THE TURN TO THE superego is not the only misstep that can befall the project of emancipation. Emancipatory politics also becomes derailed when it assumes the form of enjoyment associated with the Right. This occurs when those on the Left seek out an enemy. Emancipation always has those who oppose it, forces that want to create an oppressive structure based on their particular identity. This opposition provides a constant threat that the forces of emancipation must struggle against. There is no smooth functioning of emancipatory politics that doesn't have anyone opposing it, nor can we imagine a future emancipated state that everyone will accept. Emancipation will always have adversaries that refuse universal nonbelonging and cling to the security of their particularism.

But the adversaries of emancipation are not its enemies. This is what separates the leftist project of emancipation from the conservative attempt to constitute a community through recourse to the figure of the enemy. For the project of emancipation, the existence of an enemy signals its demise. Once one allows the adversary to become an enemy, the enjoyment of the internal contradiction has transmuted into the enjoyment of an opposition between friend and enemy. When an emancipatory project or regime takes on an enemy, it becomes a conservative project, no matter what its original intent.

This is precisely what happened in the case of the Soviet Union. The Soviet Union began as an emancipatory project. Lenin's revolution was a genuine attempt to install a communist regime that would eventually lead to global emancipation. The rest of the world was not accommodating. Surrounded by capitalist nations eager to destroy the communist experiment, the Soviet Union had adversaries everywhere, including the White movement within the nation waging a civil war against the new communist regime. But this regime did not have to erect enemies, which is what took place under Stalin's rule. Stalin cemented his control over the Soviet Union through the standard conservative mechanism of creating not just an external enemy to fight but also an internal one. Despite emerging in the midst of an emancipatory project, Stalin took up the intrinsically right-wing strategy of creating an enemy. This role fell to Leon Trotsky and then to many others.

By constructing Trotsky as an enemy, Stalin was able to deflect blame for the internal failures and contradictions of the Soviet system. The economic downturn in Stalin's Soviet Union had a clear cause in the figure of the enemy who was out to bring down the regime. Stalin made sure that his secret police saw this enemy everywhere. As Stephen Kotkin notes in his history of Stalin, "NKVD operatives would 'unmask' enemies to win raises, medals, and promotions; informants, queried about a 'Trotskyite' underground, would become eager to please."[1] The enemy became the only source of the communal bond. In this way, the leftist revolution that took place in Russia took on a rightist visage.

The imaginary construction of a Trotskyite conspiracy had the effect of creating a sense of belonging under Stalin's rule. When an enemy appears to concretize belonging, it is evident that the project of emancipation has turned into its opposite—a conservative regime. This is what we find in the Soviet Union, despite

---

1   Stephen Kotkin, *Stalin, Volume 2: Waiting for Hitler, 1929–1941* (New York: Penguin, 2017), 325.

the profound economic changes that took place there. What is ironic is that Stalin relied on the enemy to forge national unity as the project of collectivization advanced. Stalin began forced collectivization in 1928, and it continued apace until 1940, at which time a collective economy had almost fully replaced the market.

The figure of the enemy played a key role in the process of collectivization. The enemy was not just Trotsky, but every peasant who resisted becoming part of a collective farm. Stalin and his epigones invented the category of the kulak to explain peasant resistance. The kulak was an internal enemy of the regime, a peasant who refused to participate in collective farming. By propping up the kulak as the enemy, Stalin could explain why collectivization produced famine rather than plenty, misery rather than satisfaction. The internal status of this enemy enabled him to justify why things were going awry. Collectivization didn't fail on its own but did so only due to the efforts of the kulaks to sabotage the project.

Stalin's reliance on enemies such as Trotsky and the kulaks reveals the fundamentally conservative turn that the project of emancipation underwent in the Soviet Union. The fact that this turn occurred at the same time as the process of collectivization indicates that Soviet society became more communist economically as its political structure became more conservative. By attempting to use the enemy to constitute belonging to the collectivist project that the Soviet Union was undertaking, Stalin made emancipatory solidarity impossible. He politically undermined the economic trajectory that he unleashed, which suggests that forced collectivization was itself a failed economic path.

The rightward political turn that Stalin takes shows how the creation of an enemy that facilitates belonging militates against the formation of solidarity. Where people believe that they can belong, it is impossible to develop solidarity with others through nonbelonging. In his account of Stalin's Great Purge, Robert Conquest points out that one of its primary effects was the elimination of solidarity and its replacement with belonging to Stalin's regime. Conquest states, "Right through the Purge, Stalin's blows were struck at every form of solidarity and comradeship outside of that provided by personal allegiance to himself. In general, the Terror destroyed personal confidence between private citizens everywhere."[2] Stalin uses the Terror to create belonging that centers around himself, but the cost of this belonging is the destruction of the solidarity of nonbelonging, which is the heart of the emancipatory project.

While Stalin's turn away from emancipation is the ultimate one, his case is not isolated. We can see a similar trajectory, albeit not as extreme, in figures such as Maximilien Robespierre in revolutionary France and Jean-Jacques Dessalines in revolutionary Haiti. In each case, these leaders have recourse to an enemy in order to give people a community where they can belong. The lure of belonging and the sense of security it provides, both for the leader and the people, proves too difficult to forgo. Although the enemy signals a danger to the regime, this threat is much less imposing than that of universal nonbelonging, which is the structure of the emancipatory project. Making an enemy out of an adversary betrays emancipation by giving people a way to belong.

Stalin turned to the enemy as a way of solving the crisis into which the revolutionary society was plunged. The effort to collectivize led to economic hardship and famine. The enemy provided someone to blame for the crisis. Crisis always marks an inflection point in political struggle. It gives both Right and Left an opening to assert their competing forms of enjoyment. Stalin opted to use the crisis to turn the Soviet Union definitively to the Right. But crisis, especially that which occurs in capitalist society, can also lead to a turn to the Left.

---

2   Robert Conquest, *The Great Terror: A Reassessment*, 40th anniversary ed. (Oxford: Oxford University Press, 2008), 255.

15

The Opportunity
of the Crisis

CRISIS REPRESENTS AN OPPORTUNITY for both the Left and the Right. The Left can turn the crisis into a precipitous moment for emancipation if it is able to focus everyone's attention on the internal contradiction made evident. But the Right can just as easily use this occasion to foment the enjoyment of an enemy who it deems responsible for the crisis. The crisis brings out the contrast between these two approaches to contradiction.

Both the Great Depression of 1929 and the recession of 2008 show the political openness of a crisis. After the election of Franklin Roosevelt in 1932, the Great Depression became the engine for years of social change unseen in American history before or after. The economic crisis occasioned a massive public works program, a new system of retirement payments, new restrictions on capital, and relief programs for the unemployed. Roosevelt's New Deal dramatically transformed American capitalism in the direction of socialism, even if he undertook the programs in an effort to save capitalism.

Roosevelt was at times open about his hostility to the forces of big capital, though he always kept his distance from terms like *socialism* and *communism*. When he took up this position, he provided a mode of enjoyment opposed to the capitalist paradigm, which the crisis allowed him to promote. Roosevelt's mobilization of a leftist form of enjoyment reaches its apogee in a speech from

October 31, 1936, that announces the Second New Deal. In this speech, Roosevelt proclaimed,

> We had to struggle with the old enemies of peace—business and financial monopoly, speculation, reckless banking, class antagonism, sectionalism, war profiteering. They had begun to consider the government of the United States as a mere appendage to their own affairs. We know now that government by organized money is just as dangerous as government by organized mob. Never before in all our history have these forces been so united against one candidate as they stand today. They are unanimous in their hate for me—and I welcome their hatred.[1]

This speech reveals exactly why Roosevelt succeeded in transforming American society in the direction of emancipation. He provided a new way of structuring enjoyment that highlighted the contradiction between capital and the state within capitalist society. By championing the state against big capital, Roosevelt gave people a way to enjoy this contradiction.

Roosevelt's proclamation that he welcomed the hatred of the forces of big capital had the effect of enabling his listeners to envision their enjoyment differently than through the future accumulation of capital, which had become an impossible fantasy due to the crisis. By doing so, he specifically rejected a reactionary form of enjoyment. He did not appeal to national identity but to the contradiction between big capital and the ordinary people that it supposedly served, whom he as a candidate represented. Listeners could enjoy themselves through this contradiction, especially because Roosevelt located them on the proper side of it. The lesson

---

1   Franklin Roosevelt, "Address Announcing the Second New Deal," October 31, 1936.

of Roosevelt is that crisis represents an opportunity for emancipation if one mobilizes enjoyment around it in an emancipatory way that embraces contradiction rather than taking aim at an enemy.

The structure of enjoyment in Germany at the same time unfolded in the opposite way. Germany responded to the economic crisis with the election of the ultra-nationalist Nazis.[2] Although Germany never directly elected Hitler president or chancellor, the plurality of support for the Nazi Party led to his appointment and his ascension to power. He was not an unpopular figure who perpetuated a coup d'état that the people resisted. Nazis and fellow reactionary parties had the support of the German people. Their ethnic nationalist response to the crisis carried with it a promise of enjoyment that proved politically superior to the communist alternative proffered at the time.

Whereas Roosevelt organized the nation's enjoyment around the idea of standing up to big capital, Hitler fomented an ethnic nationalist enjoyment that targeted communists and Jews as the chief danger to the Aryan identity and the German nation. Nazism succeeded in Germany by providing a structure through which ordinary Germans could enjoy their ethnicity and their nation as never before. Even philosophers who should have known better became swept up in the national enjoyment that offered an explanation and a way out of the crisis. Unlike Roosevelt, Hitler did not set himself up in opposition to big capital but to Jews who were responsible for the theft of German wealth. By hating the communist and the Jew, the ordinary Germans could find a hitherto unknown way to enjoy being German.

---

2 On the basis of the popular vote, the Nazis gained a plurality in the Reichstag in 1932, a position that led President Paul von Hindenburg ultimately to appoint Hitler Chancellor of Germany in 1933. In a subsequent election in March 1933 after Hitler had been chancellor for two months, the Nazis retained their plurality in the Reichstag and their governing coalition.

The economic crisis undermines the enjoyment that the capitalist system offers. This enjoyment occurs in the process of labor and consumption driven by the promise of a perfect satisfaction to come. When this future ceases to be imaginable, the process of labor and consumption dries up, and capitalist enjoyment comes to a halt. This is why the crisis is a propitious moment for radical change and why the Left has always found solace in it.

The problem is that the response to the crisis can be a return to nationalist or ethnic enjoyment rather than that of an emancipatory alternative. Although egalitarianism might be the sensible way out of the crisis, it is not necessarily the most evidently enjoyable. For the Germans of early 1933, the nation promised more enjoyment than an emancipatory struggle, which is why the Nazis received so much more support than socialists and communists. One never knows ahead of time which path will appear as more enjoyable. This crisis is an opportunity, but it is an opportunity fraught with danger. To believe that a crisis will necessarily bring revolutionary change is to write enjoyment out of the analysis, which is the mistake that constantly beguiles the Left.

16

Capitalism's
Particular Problems

CRISIS DOES REVEAL, HOWEVER, that capitalism represents a barrier that the project of emancipation must transcend. Capitalist society inherently resists the enjoyment of contradiction that the emancipatory project takes up. Although capitalism runs into insurmountable contradictions, it constantly tries to surmount them rather than reconcile itself to them. This is why there can be no emancipated form of capitalism and no universal capitalist society.

The barrier that capitalism continually comes up against is its own inability to attain universality. It always remains mired in a particularism that it endeavors unsuccessfully to escape. This failure is how capitalism succeeds: the attempt to attain universality and the inability to do so keep the capitalist system functioning. Capitalism strives to move from the particular to the universal but never quite gets there. The capitalist system cannot become universal because it requires an external field into which it must try to expand.[1] The external field is an internal requirement of

---

1   This is a point that Rosa Luxemburg insists on in *The Accumulation of Capital*. According to Luxemburg, capitalist accumulation constitutes not just the internal structure of the capitalist system but also an external field into which it must attempt to expand. She writes, "Accumulation is not merely an internal relation between the branches of the capitalist economy—it is above all a relation between capital and its noncapitalist milieu." Rosa Luxemburg, *The Accumulation of Capital: A Contribution to the Economic Theory of Imperialism*, trans. Nicholas Gray, in *The Complete Works of Rosa Luxemburg, Volume II: Economic*

capitalism. If a barrier to universality doesn't exist, capitalism creates the barrier that it endeavors to surmount, in the same way that Amazon begins to sell groceries when it runs out of possibilities for expansion in the sale of books. The new territory represents the introduction of a new barrier to transcend after eliminating all the old ones. This is a self-defeating process because the more the system threatens to surpass the barrier, the more it reinforces it. Neither individual capitalists nor the economic system as a whole ever reaches the paradise that it promises.

The point of the capitalist drive is expansion, not universality. It never attains universality because this is never the animating force behind its development. It remains mired in particularisms that satisfy themselves through their striving and failing to become universal. This is what Marx is getting at in the third volume of *Capital* when he claims, "The *true barrier* to capitalist production is *capital itself*. It is that capital and its self-valorization appear as the starting and finishing point, as the motive and purpose of production; production is production only for *capital*, and not the reverse."[2] Because the capitalist system aims at constant self-expansion, it can never reach the universality that it seems to strive toward. As a result, contradictions beset capitalist society, but this society can never reconcile itself with contradiction, which is the project of emancipation.

It is only through universality that a society can become reconciled to contradiction rather than constantly trying to overcome it. Through universality, the enjoyment of contradiction becomes open to everyone. Everyone can be acknowledged as a member of the society only insofar as we recognize that no one belongs.

Writings 2, eds. Peter Hudis and Paul Le Blanc (London: Verso, 2015), 303. This expansion is necessary because the capitalist system, like the individual capitalist, is either expanding or dying. There is no possibility for simply sustaining the status quo, for just reproducing the social order, within capitalism.

2   Karl Marx, *Capital: A Critique of Political Economy, Volume Three*, trans. David Fernbach (New York: Penguin, 1981), 358.

This contradiction—universal membership without belonging—defines universality. A universalist society would include the recognition that contradiction is necessary and enjoyable, not an obstacle to be avoided. But this is what capitalism cannot attain.

To the capitalist subject, contradictions always appear as what one must try to overcome, not what constitutes one as a subject and makes enjoyment possible. As a capitalist, I try to accumulate in order to reach a point where I no longer suffer from the contradiction that drives me to accumulate, but this moment never comes. I seek more but never attain enough. Capitalism is always bent on attaining belonging by overcoming the basic social contradiction. Emancipation must replace the failed attempt to overcome contradiction with becoming reconciled with it. Only in this way can we achieve the universality that emancipation requires.

Emancipation must be universal because emancipation for some and not others is the formula of oppression. Capitalism's failure to be universal leaves it unable to become reconciled with contradiction. Instead, the individuals in the capitalist economy and the system as a whole constantly endeavor to overcome contradiction and attain plenitude. Plenitude is the capitalist fantasy, but capitalism works only if it leaves this fantasy unrealized. A world of plenitude would be a world incompatible with the capitalist drive to accumulate. In the capitalist universe, not only must some remain impoverished so that others can prosper, even those who attain the height of prosperity cannot accept that they have achieved plenitude. Instead, the wealthiest capitalists, not the poorest, consistently exhibit the most lust for more. Jeff Bezos must constantly seek to augment how much capital he has, even though he already has enough to support him and a nearly infinite number of descendants. Capitalist subjects and capitalist society can never have enough.

Marx analyzes this problem with capitalism in a work that he left unpublished during his lifetime, known simply as *The*

Grundrisse (or the notebooks). Although this scattered and unfinished work provides the model for the much more well-known *Capital*, there are insights in the early work that do not make it into Marx's magnum opus. Specifically, Marx formulates capitalism's failure to universalize itself in a way that he doesn't later on. He writes, "The universality towards which it [capital] irresistibly strives encounters barriers in its own nature, which will, at a certain stage of its development, allow it to be recognized as being itself the greatest barrier to this tendency, and hence will drive towards its own suspension."[3] As the capitalist strives to achieve universality, this figure continually falls back into particularity. The particularism of the capitalist system finds itself at odds with its striving toward universality. This particularism condemns this system to strive toward universality without ever having the possibility of achieving it.

The failure of capitalism to achieve universality manifests itself in a contradiction that occurs within every particular capitalist. In order to maximize the surplus value that each worker produces, the capitalist wants to pay the worker as little as possible. By doing so, the capitalist can increase the margin between what a commodity sells for and what it costs to produce that commodity. Surplus value ultimately manifests itself as profit. Minimizing the wage is crucial for profiting off the worker's labor. But a worker who earns a wage sufficient only to reproduce the worker for another day's work will not have enough money to buy a sufficient number of commodities to keep the capitalist enterprise expanding.

The problem is that for the capitalist surplus value develops in a double temporality. Initially, the worker produces surplus value for the capitalist through excess labor that the capitalist doesn't compensate (which is why it can return a surplus). But in a second moment, the capitalist must realize the surplus value that the

---

3   Karl Marx, *Grundrisse*, trans. Martin Nicolaus (New York: Penguin, 1993), 410.

worker has created through the sale of the commodity. In order to constantly expand the business, the capitalist must not simply sell what is necessary to reproduce the productive apparatus but must sell more and more. The problem is that by paying the worker only the necessary wage, the capitalist leaves the worker with no money to buy excess commodities and assist in the realization of surplus value. The one task of the capitalist runs directly against the other.

The particular interest of the capitalist comes into contradiction with the universal drive to realize surplus value. There is no possible resolution to this contradiction for the capitalist subject. In *The Grundrisse*, Marx makes this contradiction clear. He states, "Every capitalist knows this about his worker, that he does not relate to him as producer to consumer, and [he therefore] wishes to restrict his consumption, i.e., his ability to exchange, his wage, as much as possible. Of course, he would like the workers of *other* capitalists to be the greatest consumers possible of *his own* commodity."[4] How capitalists relate to their own workers is irreconcilable with how they would like to relate to workers as a whole. To take a random example, Ben and Jerry's Ice Cream wants to pay its workers as little as possible in order to maximize the surplus value that the company can generate, but at the same time, Ben and Jerry's wants Apple and Microsoft to pay their workers as much as possible so that they will have enough excess to buy an expensive brand of ice cream rather than just a generic one.

But each capitalist acts like Ben and Jerry's. None acts in the way that Ben and Jerry's wants the others to act. Each follows their particular interest and disregards the universal. Hence, workers never have enough money to keep the capitalist system out of its intermittent crises. Only by taking on debt can they do so, which gives debt the central role in maintaining capitalist society. If there are times when labor has an upper hand and unemployment is low,

---

4   Karl Marx, *Grundrisse*, 420.

this inevitably leads to a crisis of overproduction that subsequently decimates the labor market and disempowers workers.

The contradiction between the production and realization of surplus value leads to a crisis of demand—workers lack the money to buy the commodities that would keep capital expanding—and a crisis of overproduction—workers earn too much and drive up the cost of commodities so that people cannot afford to buy enough of them. These crises regularly crop up not because of mismanagement of the economy by various governments but because capitalists must pay their own workers at a rate lower than they require the workers at other companies to be paid. Capitalism is stuck in the particular despite requiring universality in order to stave off its perpetual crises. The crises are a result of capitalism's inability to attain the universality toward which it continually strives.

As Marx lays out, contradictions inhere in the capitalist system. Capitalism's oppressiveness derives from its refusal to integrate the necessity of contradiction into its structure. To be a capitalist subject is to refuse the necessity of contradiction and to invest oneself in eliminating all contradictions. This is the promise of accumulation: if one accumulates enough, one attains the enjoyment of surmounting contradiction. But this is a false conception of enjoyment, an image of enjoyment freed from lack rather than emerging out of it.

The problem with capitalism is not its contradictions. The problem lies in the inability of the capitalist system to become universal and thereby reconcile itself with contradiction instead of trying to overcome it. Capitalism's incessant efforts to move beyond contradiction through some technological or managerial leap betray its inability to come to terms with the political necessity of contradiction. Doing so would require capitalism to abandon its privileging of the particular and its disregard of the universal. Reconciling itself with contradiction would require capitalism to cease to be capitalism and to become an egalitarian system that accepted the universality of nonbelonging rather than privileging the belonging of the few at the expense of the many.

A universalist system that succeeded capitalism would not guarantee the end of all crises. Becoming reconciled with contradiction is not the path to utopia. But it would provide an appealing alternative to capitalism's particularism that remains bent on disingenuously striving after a universal that it is incapable of attaining. Emancipation arrives at universality rather than vainly pursuing it in the way that capitalist society does. In order to carve out the path to the universality that capitalism cannot integrate into its functioning, it suffices to focus on the impossible, that which has no position in the social field.

Despite promising that there is nothing one cannot have, the contemporary capitalist order actually has a circumscribed terrain of possibilities. It is not as limited as that of the Han Dynasty or the Roman Empire, but it is not bereft of impossibilities. One of the most significant impossibilities that we confront today is that of considering alternative socioeconomic systems. Contemporary capitalist society not only presents itself as the only game in town, but it also presents itself as the only possible game in town. The catastrophic failures to realize a communist society in the twentieth century serve as the justification for this position that insists on the absence of any viable alternative, which Mark Fisher calls capitalist realism.[5] But a justification is not a proof of capitalism's absolute superiority to any other possible socioeconomic system.[6]

While the failures of the Soviet Union and Cambodia may tell us something about how we should not envision a communist

---

5 Mark Fisher, *Capitalist Realism: Is There No Alternative?* (Winchester, UK: Zero Books, 2009).

6 As Alain Badiou likes to say, we have not yet invented the best socioeconomic system and should not assume that we have found it with capitalism.

future, they provide no statement at all for the definitive superiority of capitalism relative to all other systems. But this is what the proponents of capitalist realism claim. They see one type of planned economy go horribly awry, and they conclude with a negative judgment about all egalitarian economies, without ever bothering to tally the damage wrought by the unplanned capitalist economy that they champion, which now includes impending destruction that outstrips even that of the Soviet Union—rendering the planet uninhabitable for most future humans.

17

The Contradictory
Politics of Emancipation

GIVEN THEIR RESPECTIVE RELATIONS to belonging and nonbelonging, it is easier to imagine a right-wing movement in power than a leftist one. Being in power seems to imply taking up the side of belonging rather than nonbelonging. Those who are in power typically emphasize that the social order has enemies that it must defend itself against. If we add that leftists today see power as anathema, it becomes almost impossible to envision what an emancipatory power structure would look like.

And yet, it is incumbent for the project of emancipation not to confine itself to resistance, to force itself to think about what emancipation in power looks like. If one focuses all one's attention on resistance and leaves the ruling to others, one gives up on emancipation altogether. Resistance to oppressive situations is necessary, but it must include an idea of how to structure a ruling apparatus after the period of resistance. An emancipatory project that doesn't aim to rule ceases to be an emancipatory project because it will enable a conservative rule that it requires in order to have something to resist.

Even Michel Foucault, the great apostle of the resistance to power, recognizes this. Late in his life, he begins to see that resistance can become an end in itself that doesn't provide a path toward overcoming what one is resisting. Resistance alone, he comes to believe, is not enough. Foucault states, "I've become rather irritated by an attitude, which for a long time was mine, too, and which I no longer subscribe to, which consists in saying: our problem is to denounce and to criticize; let them get on with their legislation and their reforms. That doesn't seem to me the right attitude."[1] This shift in position, one might presume, is what leads Foucault back to the Greeks of Antiquity in the course of writing the *History of Sexuality*. In classical Greek society, Foucault finds a form of life that he can embrace, in contrast to the structures of modernity for which he has only critique.[2] Even if one might dispute the attractiveness of the Greek model, what stands out is Foucault's acceptance of the need for the project of emancipation to accept the responsibility of ruling rather than to remain in the position of pure resistance. One must imagine emancipation in power.

The paradigm for the emancipatory project taking power is the ending of the teen classic *Heathers* (Michael Lehmann, 1989), a film so radical it is hard to believe that the moguls in Hollywood ever permitted it to be made. *Heathers* shows the contrast between the conservative politics of opposition and the emancipatory embrace of contradiction by depicting the move from

---

1   Michel Foucault, "Confinement, Psychiatry, Prison," in *Politics, Philosophy, Culture: Interviews and Other Writings 1977–1984*, ed. Lawrence D. Kritzman, trans. Alan Sheridan, et al. (New York: Routledge, 1988), 209.

2   What Foucault appreciates about the Greece of Antiquity is its avoidance of the universal system of prohibition that develops in Christian Europe. He seeks a system of rule that is not universalist in scope, which is what he believes that he finds in Greece. He writes, "In classical thought, ... the demands of austerity were not organized into a unified, coherent, authoritarian moral system that was imposed on everyone in the same manner; they were more in the nature of a 'supplement,' a luxury in relation to the commonly accepted morality. Further, they appear in 'scattered centers' whose origins were in different philosophical or religious movements." Michel Foucault, *History of Sexuality, Volume 2: The Use of Pleasure*, trans. Robert Hurley (New York: Vintage, 1990), 21. While Foucault does move away from the position of pure resistance, his insistent association of universality with oppression marks a limit to his significance for the project of emancipation. Contra Foucault, universality is the necessary condition for emancipatory politics.

one to the other. The Heathers are a clique of girls that ruthlessly dominates Westerburg High School, ostracizing anyone who fails to conform to the dictates of popularity that they lay down. Their reign operates through brutal exclusion and the creation of a rigid opposition between insiders and outsiders. Although they inspire terror in almost all the students at the school, everyone seeks their recognition.

The Heathers enact a reign of rightist terror that annihilates anyone who emerges as an enemy. At one point, the leader of the clique, Heather Chandler (Kim Walker), announces her rule over the school by audaciously proclaiming, "They all want me as a friend or a fuck." This boast goes unchallenged because no one doubts its truth. Her mastery of the school depends on a strict barrier between who belongs and who doesn't, a barrier that Heather Chandler herself enforces. At another point, she mocks social outcast Martha Dunnstock (Carrie Lynn) by prompting her to believe a popular guy has affection for her. The subsequent embarrassment that Dunnstock experiences when the guy laughs in her face exemplifies how conservative enjoyment functions: the Heathers enjoy through those, like Martha Dunnstock, who don't belong. This enjoyment relies on the opposition that obscures nonbelonging as its true source. The clique has to guard a rigid barrier between belonging and nonbelonging in order to hide from itself the nature of its own form of enjoyment, which is that of the nonbelonging of those it attacks. As the film opens, Veronica (Winona Ryder), despite the fact that her name isn't Heather, is part of this clique. She belongs, despite her reservations about the clique's exclusivity.

The primary disruption to the reactionary regime of the Heathers occurs through the character of JD (Christian Slater). Veronica is initially drawn to JD as someone new to Westerburg who appears different than everyone else. After they hit it off, JD and Veronica visit Heather Chandler one morning when she is home alone. Proposing a hangover remedy for her, JD actually gives her drain cleaner to drink, which leads to her death. His sociopathy leads later to the deaths of two popular football players as well, whom he shoots, along with Veronica (after convincing her that they were not using actual bullets).

Veronica finally sees that he is criminally insane after initially allowing herself to be deceived by his claims that the deaths he caused were accidents. When she comes to this revelation, Veronica cuts off contact with him and sees the threat that he represents. But JD continues with his violent plans that conclude with a vision of blowing up the entire student body of the school during a pep rally. Veronica interrupts this plan by shooting him in the basement of the school. After being shot, he blows himself up in front of the school as Veronica watches. Despite JD's violent disturbance of the regime of popularity at Westerburg, after his suicide, the rule of the Heathers seems to remain intact, as Heather Duke (Shannen Doherty) continues in the position of the school's social authority, replacing the deceased Heather Chandler. But Veronica interrupts Heather Duke's rule. At the end of the film, she breaks from the clique and announces the birth of a genuinely universalist regime at the school.

Heathers concludes with Veronica taking a bright red ribbon from the hair of Heather Duke, the new Heather in charge, and telling her, "There's a new sheriff in town." It is significant that Veronica does not renounce power altogether as she breaks from the clique. Instead, she accomplishes a universalist revolution, moving from the particularist regime of the Heathers into a universalist one. Rather than exercising her newly asserted authority in a traditional way, Veronica befriends social outcast Martha Dunnstock, who was earlier the object of the derision of the Heathers (and Veronica herself). In the concluding shot of the film, we see

Veronica walking next to Martha, who is riding in a wheelchair, as she invites Martha over to her house to watch videos instead of going to the prom.

The appearance of Veronica in this scene is theoretically significant. Throughout the film, Veronica and the Heathers have been the best dressed students in the school. They set the style for the others. But in this final scene when Veronica takes power from Heather Duke and walks with Martha Dunnstock down the hall, her clothes are in tatters and her face is covered with ash from JD's explosion. Her appearance now signals her own nonbelonging, in contrast to her former appearance as one who belongs. This look reinforces Veronica's act.

The ending of *Heathers* depicts a different type of relationship to nonbelonging. In her first act as the self-proclaimed new sheriff of Westerburg, Veronica embraces Martha, the figure of nonbelonging that everyone disdains, as a figure of privilege. Unlike the reign of the Heathers or other cliques, Veronica's new reign eschews popularity for the sake of one who doesn't belong—the turn toward Martha. It is a regime centered on the embrace of contradiction and the nonbelonging that results from it. Veronica doesn't eliminate popularity or fitting in—popular students still exist at Westerburg, we should assume—but recognizes that equality is possible and exists only through the position of nonbelonging, which is why she reaches out to the ostracized and makes the last first without creating a new sense of belonging.

Emancipatory politics doesn't try to make this point of nonbelonging belong—this is what the politics of inclusivity does—but rather insists that society must organize itself around the point of nonbelonging. The contrast between a genuine emancipatory politics and the politics of inclusivity is instructive. The universalist position argues for the inclusion of nonbelonging as nonbelonging, the inclusion of this absence within the whole. In this vision of things, nonbelonging functions as a necessary hole that defines the whole. Genuine emancipation does not try to make this absence into a presence, which is what the inclusivist position does. The inclusivist position includes nonbelonging by transforming it into what can belong. It turns the proletariat into the bourgeoisie. By converting nonbelonging to belonging, inclusivism attempts to eliminate nonbelonging. It tries to create a whole without absence, a whole without a hole, a bourgeoisie without a proletariat. Emancipation insists on the hole.

While the inclusivist project sounds much better on the surface than the emancipatory one (insofar as it gets rid of this bothersome absence and the trouble of nonbelonging), it has the unfortunate effect of producing an unrelenting assault on any nonbelonging that remains. Inclusivity sees nonbelonging as the contingent product of an unjust order that it strives to eliminate. The champions of inclusivity are progressives. According to this position, if we progress far enough, we will bring about a society where nonbelonging no longer exists. It does not grant nonbelonging any existential status because it is just an error to be corrected.

Since no social order can ever reach the point of total belonging and completely eliminate nonbelonging, the politics of total inclusivity necessarily fails. No matter how many identities inclusivity manages to recognize, more will inevitably crop up that will require additional acts of inclusion. While emancipation includes failure within the structure, inclusivity encounters the necessary failure of total belonging as an external barrier, the result of insufficient education or the reluctance to accept difference. At some point, inclusivity will run aground on its own internal limitation because nonbelonging necessarily exists within every social structure. But since the politics of inclusivity doesn't admit the necessity of nonbelonging, it cannot interpret this internal limitation as internal.

The politics of inclusivity fails to internalize the joke about the perfect golf ball. In this joke, two friends are golfing, and one says to the other, "You should change to my type of golf ball because it's absolutely perfect." "How so?" says his friend. The first man states, "It's impossible to lose. If you hit it into the woods, it shines a light so that you can find it. If you hit it into the water, it automatically floats back to the shore. And if you hit it into tall grass, it emits a sound so that you can locate it." "Wow," replies the friend, who adds, "Where did you get it?" The first man responds, "I found it." As this joke shows, even the perfect golf ball that cannot be lost must have originally been lost in order to be acquired in the first place. Similarly, the politics of inclusion can be completely open to every possible position except the one that rejects its original presupposition of openness. The first gesture of inclusion, like the finding of the golf ball, must remain repressed in order for this system to function.

As a result of the inherent failure of inclusion, there is a persistence of nonbelonging, which drives inclusivists in one of two directions. Either they succumb to cynicism and give up on the prospects for substantial political change, or they turn rightward and identify an enemy within the society that makes total inclusion impossible. According to the frustrated inclusivists, this enemy is the bloc that cannot get onboard with the project of total inclusion (what Hillary Clinton calls "a basket of deplorables"). Their failure to accept the politics of inclusion licenses the elimination of their symbolic status within the society. Resistance to inclusivism justifies stripping away platforms that allow anti-inclusivists to articulate their position publicly. When the position of inclusivity takes action against an enemy in this way, it begins to turn into the conservatism that it opposes. Genuine universality cannot have an enemy, no matter how extreme its opponents are. At every step of the political struggle, it holds open the possibility for the opponent's conversion rather than insisting on the opponent's eradication.

In contrast to the politics of inclusivity, the emancipatory position argues for the significance of what doesn't belong, as Veronica does at the end of *Heathers*. If society transforms and the content of what doesn't belong changes, universalism will continue to insist on affirming nonbelonging. No social change will ever eradicate nonbelonging as a formal feature of society. But it is possible to envision a society that recognizes this formal feature as the source of all universality. What matters is the relationship that a society has to this point of nonbelonging. In their everyday functioning, most societies simply repress the point of necessary nonbelonging. They don't grant it any existence at all. They don't reckon with the fact that the perfect golf ball had to be lost in the first place.

But when a society recognizes the failure to belong as universal, it undergoes a radical change. This recognition doesn't magically eliminate all oppression within the society, but it does strip away the accepted justifications for oppression. It demands that those invested in the prejudices and inequalities of the prevailing social order confront the structural necessity that produces them. Through this imperative, universalism would make business as usual for the ruling capitalist order impossible. It would interrupt capitalism's steady advance by highlighting the internal limit that this advance cannot overcome, thereby paving the way for a more egalitarian order. Through the change that it introduces in our relation to the position of nonbelonging, the emancipatory project harkens toward a society in which those who don't belong are not left out.

Insisting on a society of nonbelonging is the result of politics taking enjoyment into account. For the Right, understanding the role that enjoyment plays clarifies the need for an enemy, which is Carl Schmitt's lasting contribution to conservative political philosophy, even if he never mentions the term *enjoyment*. For the Left, including enjoyment in the theorization of politics provides an alternative basis for egalitarianism. It is not simply a concern for justice that demands equality. The equality of universal nonbelonging provides a path for a radical enjoyment. When we can enjoy our nonbelonging, we advance to the terrain of emancipation.

Index